Ancestry of Frank Bartholomew 1900-1968

In the line of Lt. William Bartholomew and William Bartholomew of Burford, England

Caleb Bartholomew

ISBN-13: 978-1535301879

ISBN-10: 1535301872

Table of Contents

ACKNOWLEDGMENTS

George Wells Bartholomew and the great work he did on the "Record of the Bartholomew Family" and other Bartholomew's who have contributed pieces over time.

DEDICATION

This book is for my Uncle Mark Bartholomew primarily and all of the descendants of his father, Frank Bartholomew. This book will cover from Frank Bartholomew and his wife Edith Raphael and their ancestors as far back as is proven to go.

This is also dedicated to my Father, Richard Bartholomew who has been a great resource for 20th century information and beyond.

Resources for this book include page copies from George Wells Bartholomew's book, "Record of the Bartholomew Family" published by George Wells in 1885. Other sources include primarily from familysearch.org. I will include the ID number for each person included so that future curators of the Bartholomew Family will be able to link the family together with ease on familysearch.org. Other information will be included and cited as appropriate.

1 BEHIND THE NAME

George Wells Bartholomew has done some research into the name of "Bartholomew". Understanding the origins of the family name is essential for understanding the strength of the family name. It traces where we have come from and where we are now.

Bartholomew.

[1]

ORIGIN OF THE NAME BARTHOLOMEW.

Bartholomew is the English form of the Syriac name of the apostle *Bartholmai*, which is derived from *Bar*, the Syriac term, as *Ben* is the Hebrew, for *son* ; see Psalms ii, 12, translated " Kiss the Son ;" and Tholmai or Talmai

[1] Coat of Arms per George Wells Bartholomew (GWB)

(the same in Hebrew) is often found in the Old Testament, see Numbers xiii, 22; Joshua xv, 14; 2 Samuel iii, 3 and Chronicles xiii, 37, as Talmai. Its signification is "*furrowed*" from a Hebrew root meaning "*to furrow*" or "*cut.*"

The process by which Bartholmai or Bartalmai in Hebrew becomes Bartholomew in English, is through the regular Greek and Latin forms Bartholomaeos and Bartholomæus, the second *o* being an intercalation, thence *possibly* through the French. The Latin *ae* being treated as a simple *ē*, as in all the other Romance languages.

There are other Greek names with similar endings which have been anglicised by the use of the termination *ew*, as *Mathaios* and *Andreas* which have become Mathew and Andrew; while *Alphaios* and *Thaddaios*, not having been adopted as English names, were retained in their Latin form, the early knowledge of all Bible names being through the Vulgate translation. Zebedaios probably followed the French form and became Zebedee.

The processes by which these changes were made are so numerous and varied, as the principles of analogy, ease of utterance, and so many other natural and social forces, that, with the necessary ignorance of the peculiar history of this word during that early transitory period, it cannot now be stated just what influences gave it its present form.

ADOPTION OF THE NAME BARTHOLOMEW.

Our name has been adopted by all people who have become Christianized, because it was the name of one of Christ's apostles. Even among savages wherever missionaries have introduced the Christian religion, the names of the apostles have been given as baptismal names.

Probably the first Bartholomew in the state of Connecticut, which nearly all of the name in the United States have considered their ancestral home, was an Indian chief who, with his fellow chief Neguitimaug, deeded to the English settlers the land upon which the town of Sharon is situated. He was undoubtedly converted by some early Christian missionary and christened Bartholomew; which is a fair illustration of the manner in which the thousands of others originally adopted the name.

In England, the adoption of family names was at first confined to the nobility, but later as the common people began to accumulate property and became better informed they chose family names. The English Church, after its establishment (1538), required the parishes to keep a record of all baptisms, marriages and burials, which permanently established family names.

In Germany, the adoption of surnames among the common people was still later than in England.

Wherever the name Bartholomew has been introduced, it has suffered numerous changes and contractions, the more ignorant the people the greater the number.

I will mention a few of the English family names that have been made from it, according to those who study their origin; and the immense number which have been derived from it by other people can be imagined. They are as follows: Barthelemy, Bartholow, Barth, Bartlett, Bartelot, Bartle, Bartie, Batt, Batts, Bate, Bates, Batson, Bateson, Batey, Batty, Battye, Battcock, Badcock, Badkin, Batkin, etc.

The spelling of the name by the ancestors of the American families was as given in the references to them.

PRONUNCIATION.

THE pronunciation of our name has been as varied as the people using it. The apostles no doubt accented the first syllable, as with them it had its special meaning, and pronounced it *Bar'-tol-mā'*.

The family in Warborough, England, were, judging by the spelling in the records, in 1500, called "*Bar-tyl-mĭ*," and that vulgar pronunciation continued down to the present century.

The hill in Ipswich, Mass., named after William Bartholomew of that place (1634 ?), and the pond near Salem, Mass., named after his brother Henry, are still called *Bar′-tyl-mĭ Hill* and *Bar′-tyl-mĭ Pond*.

But educated English and American members have probably always called themselves *Bar-thol′-o-mew*.

Because the name is long and difficult to pronounce it has usually been mispronounced, and many have on that account changed it, as the great number of similar shorter family names in all nations shows.

In this country there has been but one change, so far as known; the Bartholow (*Bar-thŏ-low′*) family are descended from a German emigrant named Bartholome.

Different nations spell and pronounce the name regularly, as follows:

	Spelled.	Pronunciation.
Greek	βαρθολομαίος	Bar-thöl-o-ma′hee-os.
Latin	Bartholomæus	Bar-thöl-o-ma′hee-aos.

in which ai Greek and æ Latin have the same sound, viz.: that of a′hee or that of *ai* in English *aisle*.

Italian	Bartholomeo	Bar-tol′-o-mā′-o.
French	Bartholomée Bartholomieu.	Bar-tol′-o-mā′.
Spanish	Bartolomeo	Bar-tol′-o-mā′.
Portuguese	Bartolomeu	
German	Bartholomaeus	Bar-tol′-o-mā′-us.
Russian	Varfolomei	
Polish	Bartlomiei.	
Danish	Bartholomeuis.	

SAINT BARTHOLOMEW.

It is interesting to review what is known concerning the man from whom indirectly our name *Bartholomew* has been given to hundreds of thousands of persons, and especially to our ancestors and ourselves.

Bartholomew was not a family name, but was patronymical and meant the *son of Tholmai or Talmai*, like Barjona and Bartimæus. Possibly the original designation "son of Tholmai," was afterwards converted into an apostolic name, implying *son of a furrowed* field or cultivated fruit.

Our knowledge of the apostle is very slight and only such as the Acts of the Apostles (i, 13) and the four Gospels (Matt. x, 3; Mark iii, 18; Luke vi, 14; John i, 45-49, xxi, 2) contain. He is really never mentioned in the last Gospel by this name, but is supposed to be the same as the Nathanael (meaning *gift of God*) mentioned by Saint John.

The identity of the two was never thought of by the early church, and Augustine discusses the question why Nathanael was not chosen one of the Twelve. The idea was probably first suggested in the twelfth century by Rupert of Deutz, and the reasons for it seem sufficient. They are these: that Nathanael's vocation coördinated with that of the apostles as of equal significance; that on one occasion we meet him in the midst of the apostles, some named before him and some after (John xxi, 1, 2); that the three earlier evangelists never mention Nathanael, the fourth, as stated before, never Bartholomew, while Philip and Bartholomew are grouped together as friends, but with Philip first as he was first chosen (Matt. x, 30; Mark iii, 18); that the custom of double names seems to have been almost universal at that time in Judea, so that all, or well nigh all, the apostles bore more than one. All these arguments in favor of the identity with nothing against it, bring it very near to a certainty.

The first three Gospels and the "Acts of the Apostles" only mention Bartholomew as an apostle without any other allusion or incident from which his personal character can be imagined.

But Saint John (xxi, 2) says that Nathanael was of Cana in Galilee and in his account of the choosing of Nathanael (i, 43–49) gives us a grand portrait of him.

"43 The day following Jesus would go forth into Galilee, and findeth Philip, and saith unto him, Follow me.

44 Now Philip was of Bethsaida, the city of Andrew and Peter.

45 Philip findeth Nathanael, and saith unto him, We have found him, of whom Moses in the law, and the prophets, did write, Jesus of Nazareth, the son of Joseph.

46 And Nathanael said unto him, Can there any good thing come out of Nazareth? Philip saith unto him, Come and see.

47 Jesus saw Nathanael coming to him, and saith of him, Behold an Israelite indeed, in whom is no guile!

48 Nathanael saith unto him, Whence knowest thou me? Jesus answered and said unto him, Before that Philip called thee, when thou wast under the fig tree, I saw thee.

49 Nathanael answered and saith unto him, Rabbi, thou art the Son of God; thou art the King of Israel."

Some ancient writers, living three hundred years after his time, have mentioned his preaching the gospel in India and Arabia. Modern students think it a mistake, but acknowledge the possibility of his having preached at Hierapolis in Syria, and through Armenia and of his having suffered martyrdom at Albana or Albanapolis, the modern Derbend, on the shore of the Caspian Sea.

These, and numerous other less probable opinions, are all founded upon tradition and little reliance should be placed upon them.

There was a gospel which was attributed to St. Bartholomew, mentioned by Origen and St. Jerome, but Pope Gelasius I placed it among the apocryphal books.

His festival day in the Roman Church is Aug. 24, and in the Greek, June 11.

B

Chapter 2 The Legend Begins

The following chapter is conjecture about the Bartholomew Surname in England. It is important, however, because the logical conclusion would be that the origin of the surname is in honor of Bartholomew de Badlesmere. The people are real but how they connect to our line is what is in question.

When this chapter first began its conception, 1275 was as far back as it could go. However after additional research, two things have been concluded. Dates prior to 1275 can be proven and the probability that Frank Bartholomew is a descendent of these Bartholomew's has increased.

The first of these was Bartholomew of Badlesmere born in 1145 AD. He was born in the Tong Castle in the town of Tong, Kent, England. He was likely related to whoever the custodian of the castle was as three generations were born here. There is not whole lot of information surrounding him.[2] From what will be revealed with the next Bartholomew, it is likely Bartholomew was a Surname or became a surname afterwards.

Because a few Bartholomew's were born in the Tong

---

[2] http://www.armidalesoftware.com/issue/full/ , Washington, 2016. *Ancestral File*, CD-ROM database (Salt Lake City: The Church of Jesus Christ of Latter-day Saints, 1998)

Castle it will be important to discuss the castle and some of the history.

It is likely that Tong Castle was one of the castles William the Conqueror built as it dates back to the eleventh century. It was built as a fortress with a tower. The purpose was to hold the progress in the conquest of England. The Earl of Montgomery lived there during that time.[3]

During the time of the first Bartholomew was born, the Castle had become more fortified under King Stephen.[4]

The second Bartholomew of Badlesmere was also born in Tong Castle. He is the first showing Bartholomew as a Surname. His name was Lord William Bartholomew de Badlesmere. Some sources list him as William de Badlesere and some Bartholomew de Badlesmere. He lived from about 1184 to 1222.[5] He was married to Margaret Montefex and was one of nineteen children.[6] While most sources have William as the second of Badlesmere, Long Island Surnames have William's father as Bartholomew born in 1161. This is likely the case as there would have been 40 years between the first and second generation. Even with 20

---

[3] http://www.discoveringtong.org/castlec11.htm This article forms part of Alan Wharton's Report No. 4 on the Tong Castle excavation published in September 1986.

[4] ibid

[5] http://www.findagrave.com/cgi-bin/fg.cgi?page=gr&GRid=132845283

[6] Citation needed

siblings it is unlikely that his mother would have had that many children aging into her 60s. Bartholomew was also born in Tong Castle in 1161 and died in 1256.[78] Gendex misses William's generation however, but multiple sources include William and again, without William's generation there are 40 years from 1161 to Giles Bartholomew III.

William Bartholomew was father to Sir Giles Bartholomew III de Badlesmere who was born in 1202 and died in 1248. He married Margaret de Leveland whom he preceded in death when he battled with Wales in 1248.[9]

A personal theory of the author is that Giles Bartholomew III had III as a suffix, not because he was the third Giles but because he was the third to use the surname Bartholomew. While many believe de Badlesmere was the last name, if Bartholomew was the first name de Badlesmere only tells where they are from. There were other Sir Bartholomew's throughout England. Using de Badlesmere identifies specifically which Bartholomew.

Giles and Margaret had a son Guncelin. It is said that he was the son of the Bartholomew who died in 1248 but his

---

[7] Longislandsurnames.com, Personal ID I07629, Family ID F06280, Gendex S015150 26 July 2016

[8] Whiting, William, "Memoir of Rev. Samuel Whiting DD and Elizabeth St. John", Boston, 1873 pp. 40

[9] Ibid footnote 5

birth date is in dispute. He was either born in 1244 or 1232. He married Joan ZitzBernard and they had two children. One child is known in history simply as Bartholomew, Baron of Badlesmere and Maud who married Sir Robert De Burghersh.[10]

Bartholomew, Baron of Badlesmere lived from 1275 AD – 1322. As a Baron, he was a soldier, a Member of Parliament, landowner and nobleman. He was the born of and heir to Sir Gunselin Badlesmere Joan Fitz Bernard. In service to Edward the first, Bartholomew fought in the English army.[11] He also fought in the earlier part of the reign of Edward II. Bartholomew was killed in an attempt to take out the Earl of Lancaster.

Bartholomew's life related to his service in Royal Army, which his earliest recorded campaigns are in Gascony in 1294, Flanders around 1297 and Scotland between the years 1298-1319.[12]

Bartholomew was not just a soldier in his young age. The King commissioned him as a diplomatic agent under the auspice of the Earl of Lincoln, sent to Rome. The Earl of

---

[10] http://www.findagrave.com/cgi-bin/fg.cgi?page=gr&GRid=75801363

[11] One or more of the preceding sentences incorporates text from a publication now in the public domain: *Chisholm, Hugh, ed. (1911). "Badlesmere, Bartholomew, Baron". Encyclopædia Britannica* ***3*** *(11th ed.). Cambridge University Press.*

[12] Simpkin, David (2008). *The English Aristocracy at War: From the Welsh Wars of Edward I to the Battle of Bannockburn*. Woodbridge. pp. 54 and 122

Lincoln brought its grievances against Scotland to Pope Boniface VIII.[13][14][15]

Other accomplishments of Bartholomew include his service in Parliament as a Knight representative of Kent.[16] He also served as the governor of the castle at Bristol. He also rebelled against the kingship and took charge of the castle.[17]

Bartholomew de Badlesmere served the King in many more capacities. With his marriage to Roger Mortimer's daughter, the King granted Bartholomew the Castle and Manor at Leeds for him and his heirs.[18] This is the final male heir in this line of de Badlesmere.

The next important Bartholomew name was

---

[13] Calendar of Close Rolls, 1296-1302, p. 370

[14] J. S. Hamilton, 'Lacy, Henry de, fifth earl of Lincoln (1249-1311)', Oxford Dictionary of National Biography, Oxford University Press, 2004; online edn, Jan 2008

[15] Calendar of Inquisitions Post Mortem, 1st series, Vol. 4, No. 38. Shortly after the return from Rome Bartholomew's father dies and Bartholomew becomes legal heir.

[16] Calendar of Close Rolls, 1302-1307, pp. 524-25

[17] Haines, Roy Martin (2003). *King Edward II: Edward of Caernarfon His Life, His Reign and Its Aftermath, 1284-1330*. Montreal: McGill-Queen's University Press. p. 99

[18] *Holmes, GA (1957). The Estates of the Higher Nobility in Fourteenth-Century England. Cambridge: Cambridge University Press. pp. 43–44.*; Calendar of Patent Rolls, Edward II, Vol. 3 (1317-1321), p. 46., p. 128.

Bartholomew de Burghersh, the First Baron. The most notable artifacts about Bartholomew de Burghersh is he was name for his uncle Bartholomew de Badlesmere and married a Mortimer, a relative of Bartholomew de Badlesmere's wife.

Edward II reneged on his offer of the Castle at Leeds when Badlesmere's wife did not allow the queen a visit. Badlesmere was killed but Burghersh was spared and imprisoned in the Tower of London. He was spared Queen Isabella whom Badlesmere's wife shut out with the intent of using him to overthrow Edward II.

He fought in France. He was an advisor. He was given land. He was more diplomatic than the man for whom he was named. When he died in 1355, he was buried at St. Catherine's in Lincoln with his brother, Robert, Bishop of Lincoln.[19]

His son, Bartholomew the second Baron of Burghersh, succeeded him as Baron of Burghersh. The English nobleman and warrior was born around 1329 and died in 1369. Bartholomew followed his father's call to military service and surpassed him in valor. His first military expedition was in 1339 in France as one of the early campaigns in the Hundred Years War. Three years later he was involved in battle in Brittany. In 1346 he was in the

[19] This article incorporates text from a publication now in the public domain: *Venables, Edmund (1886). "Burghersh, Bartholomew (d.1355)". In Stephen, Leslie. Dictionary of National Biography* **7.** *London: Smith, Elder & Co. pp. 333-334*

entourage of Edward the Black Prince in Crecy and then in the battle of Calais in 1347. Over the next decade he was involved in many more battles, his fame spread with his military prowess. He fought alongside his father and was involved in the same battle, which took his father's life. From his success in war, he was given large sums of land and when he father had died, he inherited the lands his father acquired

After his tenure on the battlefield he began his career as an ambassador for the next decade or so. At his death per his request he was buried in Walsingham Abbey.

He married Cecily de Weyland and they had one daughter, Elizabeth Burghersh. Cecily had passed and he remarried and they had no more children.[20]

Elizabeth's line can be well traced but for the purposes here is not necessary.

Trace back to Bartholomew the first Baron of Burghersh; his brother was the Henry, the Bishop of Lincoln. He had an additional residence in Ewelme, England, the Burghersh manor.[21] He was also appointed Lord Treasurer of

---

[20] Public domain: Venables, Edmund (1886): "Burghersh Bartholomew d. 1369"

[21] http://www.angelfire.com/mi4/polcrt/Burghersh.html Sypniewski, Margaret: BFA 1997

England,[22] the third highest-ranking office in England.[23] The Bishop lived from 1292 to 1340.[24]

Bartholomew de Burghersh 2nd Baron of Burghersh, John who inherited the Burghersh manor in Ewelme.[25] John owned land in six counties. His parents had died while he was young and he was not able to secure his inheritance until he was twenty-three years old. He was born in 1343 and died substantially wealthy in 1391. He had two daughters. Margaret, fifteen years old, married John Arundell II. Maud was twelve when he died and was not yet married, but she married Thomas Chaucer son of Geoffrey Chaucer.[26]

The manor was kept in the family line until the descendants of Arundell's daughter (La Poles) were tried for treason against Henry VII and executed by Henry VIII. The manor was surrendered back to the king but while it was still in the La Poles possession, it is rumored that Henry VII impregnated his wife at the Burghersh Manor in 1490 while they visited.

---

[22] Encyclopedia Britannica and EB Pryde, et al. *Handbook of British Chronology,* Cambridge 1996 p. 105

[23] http://www.merriam-webster.com/dictionary/lord%20high%20treasurer%20of%20England

[24] Ibid angelfire.com

[25] ibid

[26] http://www.historyofparliamentonline.org/volume/1386-1421/member/burghersh-sir-john-1343-91

Henry VIII and Ann Boleyn visited the manor and did not like it but they kept it as a hunting home. The manor was rescinded to the king at that point.[27]

What was the point of going through the Badlesmere family and the Burghersh family? Both family lines come to the point where there are no more male heirs to carry on the family name. These families are important to Frank Bartholomew, as they are an insight into the family tree. William de Badlesmere's generation is the key as there are eighteen other siblings whose lines we know nothing about for 400 years.

One thing we saw with this study is how even when

[27] http://onthetudortrail.com/Blog/anne-boleyn-places/palaces-and-houses/ewelme-manor/ 2016 : References & Sources
Ewelme Primary School
Ewelme, St Mary the Virgin Church
http://www.fordsfarm.co.uk/Ewelme-IV.html
National Monuments Record
Emery, A. Greater Medieval House of England and Wales: Volume III, 2006.
Starkey, D. Six Wives: The Queens of Henry VIII, 2003.
Photo on prior page copyright by fabhappysnapper

property may be taken from one family member, someone else in the family may be granted it later. With the additional siblings from Badlesmere that we do not know, they were likely still in politics and given land in Oxfordshire.

Some say that the Bartholomew's were tied to the Bishop of Lincoln. Prior to those who we are certain are in the line of Frank Bartholomew, Henry Burghersh, nephew of Bartholomew de Badlesmere, was Bishop of the Lincoln Diocese. At the time the Lincoln Diocese included Oxfordshire and Henry Burghersh owned much land in Oxfordshire. He was given his position and return land, which was forfeited, from Bartholomew de Badlesmere. He had his land taken from him because of dealings with Mortimer and Isabella. Mortimer in this case was a direct heir to the Badlesmere Estates as he married the granddaughter of Bartholomew.[28] He was Roger Mortimer, the 1st Earl of March. His land was disposed and not returned. This is where I believe we enter distant relatives become the Bartholomew surname we know.

28

http://karlwilcox.com/holc/index.php?title=Biography_of_Bishop_Henry_Burghersh

Chapter 3 The Bartholomew's of England

The first Bartholomew we have record of is William Bartholomew who was born in 1425. There is very little we know about William Bartholomew. There is nothing known about his wife except that she was born in 1429. She is only known to the author as Lady Bartholomew. There is not any additional information known to the author about this generation of the Bartholomew's. Insight can be garnered based on what is known about the following generations[29].

William and Lady Bartholomew had Sir John Bartholomew who was born in 1450. He is likely from Badlesmere, at the very least Kent. Little else is known about him.[30]

John Bartholomew II would have been born in 1472. There is a theory that he was on an envoy in 1511 with William Symond but most sources have him dying in 1501.[31] His wife, Mary Layton also died in 1501. There is little known

[29] Familysearch.org the app, Salt Lake City: ID L2TR-2ZZ added by Cassie Hartson, 2016

[30] Source unknown. The source was seen by this author in a publication but the publication has since been lost.

[31] Plomer, Henry Kent Records Index of Wills and Administrations Volume VI, 1920 p33 shows his last will and testament date from his home in Throwley, Kent, England. At this time, a will was not entered unless one was old or near death.

about here as well other than soft sources. The one thing known for sure about John Bartholomew is that he was buried in Throwley, Kent, England at St. Michael and All Angels churchyard.[32] The proximity of St. Michael to Badlesmere was close. It was one of two churches equidistant to Badlesmere. This proximity has the likelihood he was from Badlesmere which closes in the theory he was a descendant of Bartholomew of Badlesmere uncle of Bartholomew of Burghersh. One source not worth citing, said that John and Mary likely died of the black plague but that would have been historically inaccurate. If they both died of a plague in 1501 it would have likely been sweating sickness though this would have been off cycle from major outbreaks it could have happened.[33] It was common to happen within the household like that as Charles and Henry Brandon, Dukes of Suffolk died within hours of each other.[34]

John Bartholomew III was born in 1499. He would have been twelve at the time of William Symond's voyage to Aragon. As an orphaned child at the age of two, and born to a family of stature, it's likely he was taken in by others of

---

[32] Duncan, Leland: *Testamenta Cantiana: A Series of Extracts from Fifteenth and Sixteenth Century Wills Related to Church Buildings and Topography. West Kent.* London, 1906 pp. 341-342

[33] Roberts, L (1945). "Sweating Sickness and Picardy Sweat". *British Medical Journal*. **2** (4414): 196. doi:10.1136/bmj.2.4414.196. PMC 2059547 from the Wikipedia entry for sweating sickness.

[34] https://en.wikipedia.org/wiki/Sweating_sickness 2016

nobility. While he would have been young, it was not uncommon for youth to assist in expeditions such as this.[35]

William Symond was the son of a prominent beer man, who likely sat in the House of Commons, and his name: Andrew Symond. William went into ministry so while named as an heir, did not continue in the same work as his father.[36]

Sources say in 1511 William and John were in an envoy in the Hundred Years War with France. Perhaps it was religious in nature or it was easier to send a man of cloth through France to modern Spain during a conflict. The envoy went right to the Kingdom of Aragon[37] which is where Catherine Tudor, wife of Henry Tudor (Henry VIII) before any Boleyn sister were involved.

If you remember, Henry VIII rescinded the Burghersh manor into the possession of the King after the La Poles were tried. The La Poles being heirs of the Burghersh estates from Bartholomew de Burghersh, nephew of

---

[35] Ibid angelfire.com

[36] http://www.historyofparliamentonline.org/volume/1509-1558/member/symonds-william-1480-1547-or-later **Published in *The History of Parliament: the*Published in *The History of Parliament: the House of Commons 1509-1558*, ed. S.T. Bindoff, 1982 Available from** Boydell and Brewer

[37] Ibid angelfire: Source: Loade, David. *Chronicles of the Tudor Kings*. Wayne, New Jersey: BHB International Inc, 1990, 114

Bartholomew de Badlesmere. It had been common practice remit property back to the king and then be given back to the next of kin in prominent standing for example with the Bartholomew of Badlesmere and his wife not allowing the Queen to stay at the Castle Leeds. Their children were able to retain spot as heirs once they proved loyalty to the King. This was also how Henry de Burghersh, Bishop of Lincoln and custodian of the manor in Ewelme retained his land.

The theory of the author is that the Burghersh Manor in Ewelme would have been given back to the next in the Bartholomew de Badlesmere line. Since William de Badlesmere had eighteen other siblings perhaps it was down one of his siblings lines. Because John Bartholomew played an integral role in the envoy to Aragon, even so young, the Manor could have been given to him. As noted prior, Henry VIII did not like the manor too much other than as a place to hunt. Perhaps it was given purely as custodial for upkeep when Henry VIII came to visit as a Manor that size would need fulltime care.

John married Alice Scudder in Warborough in 1525. Warborough is within walking distance of the Manor in Ewelme. Perhaps it was not granted to him until after Ann Boleyn's reign ended eleven years later.

John Bartholomew IV was the heir apparent to the Burghersh Manor in Ewelme whether his father resided there or not. He is known as John Bartholomew of Burghersh.[38]

[38] Matthews, John, "Complete American Amory and Bluebook: Combining 1903, 1907 and 1911-1923 editions" Genealogical Publishing Company, 1991 Baltimore p. 203 Some would say that John Bartholomew who was born in 1472 was John Bartholomew of Burghursh had he been on the envoy. Again this is not the case per the records here since he died a decade prior.

THE BARTHOLOMEW FAMILY.

I JOHN, II ROBERT, III RICHARD,

OF ENGLAND.

THREE Bartholomews bearing above names were living in Warborough,* Oxfordshire, England, about 1550; the latter two are known to have been brothers, and it is supposed that the former also held the same relationship, from the fact that his son was made an overseer in Richard's will, while Robert's several and competent sons were still living. They held land in their own names, were church wardens, etc.

They frequently used the term "alias Martyn" (Martin) after Bartholomew, but no light has been thrown on the reason of its use. It may have arisen from the fact that they or their forefathers had inherited an estate through a maternal ancestor of that name, and it may be that they used the name to honor a distinguished ancestor named Martin Bartholomew, as, in a subsequent generation, William Bartholomew of the University of Oxford (see page 15) used the suffix "als Isaac," in honor of his worthy grandfather Isaac Bartholomew (IX).

I John[Eng. 1] Bartholomew, married, second (?), in Warborough, 22 Nov., 1551, Alice Skutter.† No record is

* See description under head of Oxfordshire.

† Was she related to Elizabeth Scudder (daughter of Thomas Scudder of Boston, Mass.) who married about 1640, (No. 2) Henry Bartholomew of Salem, Mass?

(3)

found of his death or of his will. It may have been his widow Alice who married in Warborough, 28 Sept., 1568, John Weller.

The names of his children are uncertain, except the following, mentioned as such in the record of his marriage.

iv i John[Eng. 2], m. 6 Nov., 1552, Margaret Joyes.

IV John[Eng. 2] (*John*[Eng. 1],) married in Warborough, 6 Nov., 1552, Margaret Joyes, and was probably the John buried in Warborough, 14 Nov., 1578. She may have been buried in W., 20 Sept., 1578.

He was made overseer of his uncle Richard's estate by the latter's will in 1577. He or his son John probably assisted in the founding of Bartholomew Chapel, Burford.*

His four sons apparently all settled in the neighboring towns of Oxford and Burford: Rowland in Oxford, and John, Richard and William in Burford. Children:

xi i John [Eng. 3] christened 19 June, 1556; married 12 Nov., 1593, Ales Vicarage. He is supposed to have been one of the founders of Bartholomew Chapel in Burford.

ii Rowland, christened in Warborough 5 Dec., 1561 (twin); d. in Oxford in 1587. The record of wills contains the following mention of his estate. "Administra° omnium et singularum bonorum etc., etc., Rowlandi Bartlemewe de civitati Oxon etc. granted 5 Sept., 1587 to John Wheeler† prox contang."

iii Richard, christened in Warborough, 5 Dec., 1561 (twin); m. 1st, 13 Nov., 1587, Margaret Munford; 2nd, Anne ———, who d. in Fullbrooke, 7 May, 1617; and 3rd, in F., 28 July, 1619, Elizabeth Wilkins; and was buried in Burford, 29 Apr., 1632.

xii iv William, christened 7 Feb., 1567; buried 6 May, 1634.

XII William$^{Eng. 3}$ (*John*$^{Eng. 2}$, *John*$^{Eng. 1}$,) christened in Warborough, Eng., as *Willm Bartylmewe*, 7 Feb., 1567–8; married, Friswide, daughter of William Metcalfe,* and died in Burford, Eng., and was buried as *Mr William Bartholomew, Senior*, in (?) Bartholomew Chapel, St. John's Church, Burford, 6 May, 1634.

Mrs. Friswide, who survived him and was bequeathed rooms and support in their Burford home, was mentioned by her son Richard in his will, in 1645, and was buried in Fulbrooke, 10 Dec., 1647, as "widdow of Mr William Bartholmew, Senior."

Mr. Bartholomew was a mercer, a dealer in silks and woollens, in Burford.

His long and interesting will, following, is so peculiar that it may be considered to have originated with him, and his character be judged accordingly.

The invariable prefixing of "Mr." to his name wherever used shows that he held the social rank of gentleman.

---

* He was mayor of New Woodstock. Will made 5 Dec., 1607, proved 4 Mar., 1607–8, makes behests to the church, maintenance of the preacher, to the poor of New Woodstock, Bissetir and Tame ("where I was born"), [near Warborough] sons Thomas ("mansion house" etc.), William ("my new house," etc.), daughters "Friswide Bartholmewe of Burforde," Elizabeth Trulocke, Anne Bradshawe, Johane and Margaret Metcalf, sister Ursula Noble, nephews Nathaniel and William Noble, brother Nicholas Metcalfe's children.

Extracted from the Principal Registry of the Probate Divorce and Admiralty Division of the High Court of Justice.

SOUTH EAST VIEW OF ST. JOHN'S CHURCH*, BURFORD, ENGLAND, SHOWING BARTHOLOMEW CHAPEL.

In the Prerogative Court of Canterbury.

In the Name of God Amen. The five and twentieth day of Aprill in the yeare of our Lord God one thousand sixe hundred thirty and fower and in the tenth yeare of the Raigne of our Soveraigne lord Charles by the Grace of God of England Scotland Fraunce and Ireland King Defender of the Faith &c. I William Bartholomewe the

* For the illustration of the ground plan of this church, see plate opp. p. 653.

Elder of Burford in the county of Oxon Mercer doe make and ordayne this my last Will and Testament in manner and forme following that is to say First I comend my Soule to the handes of Almighty God my Creatour hopeing and assuredly trusting by the death and blood shedding of my Lord and Saviour Jesus Christ to have full remission of all my sins and to have life everlasting my body I comend to the earth to be buryed in the Church of Burford aforesaid at the discrecon of myne Executo^s and overseers hereafter named And concerning my worldly estate I devise and bequeath it as followeth first I give towards the reparacons of the said Church of Burford tenn shillinges to be payd to the Church wardens thereof within one moneth next after my decease and alsoe I give to the poore of the Parish of Burford aforesaid twenty shillinges to be distributed amongst them by my Executour and Overseers within one moneth next after my decease Item I give and bequeath unto Richard Bartholomew my fourth sonne fifty poundes of lawfull money to be payd to him within three yeares next after my decease Item I give and bequeath unto Frauncis Bartholomew my fift sonne fifty pounds of like money to be alsoe payd to him within fower yeares next after my decease Item I give and bequeathe unto Thomas Bartholomew my sixth sonne fifty poundes of like money to be alsoe payd him within five yeares next after my decease Item I give and bequeath unto Henry my third sonne fifty pounds of like money to be alsoe payd to him within two yeares next after my decease Item I give vnto Abraham my seaventh sonne the summe of fifty poundes of like money to be payd unto him at his age of twenty and fower yeares Item I give unto Sarah my youngest daughter fifty poundes of like money to be alsoe paid to her at her age of twenty and one yeares and if any of the same my children Richard Francis Thomas Henry Abraham or Sara shall dye before their said stocks or legacyes shall be vnto them due then I will the said stocks or legacyes of him her or them soe dying shall be divided to and amongst the residue and survivours of my said children Richard Henry Francis Thomas Abraham and Sarah to be payd as their other legacyes are herin appoynted to them Item I give unto Friswide my wife for three score yeares if shee live soe long the tenement barne landes arrable meadowes and commons lying and being in Fullbrooke in the County of Oxon comonly called Hollowayes wch I lately tooke of Thomas Cambrey Item I give unto her soe much iron brasse and pewter as my Overseers shall esteeme worth fower poundes and shee to chose what iron brasse and pewter shee will have to that value and alsoe I give vnto her one bed stead with one feather bedd and one flocke bed one paire of blanckette two paire of sheets one cover ledd one feather boulster one flock boulster one paire of curtaynes two pillows pillow beeres with cordes and matt and roddes to the bed stead and she herselfe to take her choyce of the bed stead and of the rest of the furniture to her herein bequeathed at her pleasure Item I give more vnto the said Friswede my wife to be yearely issuing and receaved out of my lands in Burford the full somme of eight poundes an yeare to have and to hould the same eight poundes an yeare to her dureing her naturall life and if she refuse the same eight poundes an yeare then I leave her to her owne choice to take her dower of my landes but not to have the saide eight poundes an yeare and her said dower both Item I give unto her the Crosse Chamber and closett therevnto adioyneing and the cock loft over the same Chamber being all parcell of my now dwelling howse dureing her naturall life with passage to itt through the parlour and passages waters and other easements in the backe sides and garden of my said dwelling howse Item I give unto my daughter Mary tenn shillinges to buy her a ring and unto Merryall her daughter tenn shillinge unto Katherine John Anne Richard and Isabell alsoe her children sixe shillinge eight pence a peece to be payde unto them within sixe monethes next after my decease Item I give unto Elizabeth Sondely my late servant ten shillinge to be payd her within sixe monethes next after my decease Item I give unto Anne Monny my now servant ten shillinges to be payd her att the end of her apprentishippe Item I give unto Richard Deareing my now servant tenne shillinges to be payd him at his departure from dwelling with my Executour herein named and my will and mynd is that my Executour shall give unto my Overseers in their own names sufficient security by his owne bond for the payment of the same stock of money given to my fore named children Item my will is that my Executo[rs] shall breade up at his owne charge my twoe children Abraham and Sarah vntill their severall ages afore said and att his like charges place them in some honest vocations by and with the consent of my wife and Overseers Item I give unto my eldest sonne John Bartholomewe my howse and landes with all the appurtennces wherein I dwell in Burford afore said to have and to hould ye same to him and his heires of his body lawfully to be begotten and for default of such issue I give the same landes to Henry Bartholomew my third sonne and to the heires of his body lawfully to be begotten and for default of such issue I give the same landes to Abraham Bartholomewe my seaventh sonne and to the heires of his body lawfully to be begotten and for default of such issue the remainder of the same landes to be to the right heires of me the said Willyam Bartholomew the elder for ever All the rest of my goodes and cattells whatsoever my debtes legacyes and funerall charges being payd and discharged I doe give and bequeath vnto the said John Bartholomew my eldest sonne which said John I doe hereby ordaine and make my sole Excuto[r] of this my Testament and last Will and I doe require him vpon my blessing and upon that love w[ch] he oweth mee to performe this my Will in all thinges according to my trust to him herein com̃itted and I make and ordaine my loving kinsman William Bartholomew [see page 17] the younger and my loving friend David Hewes alias Lloyd the Overseers of this my last Will and Testament whome I doe desire to undertake the same and to performe the trust to them by me herein com̃itted for the benefitt of my children and better performance of the same my Will and I doe give to each of them for their paynes therein sixe shillinges and eight pence In wittness whereof I have herunto set my hand and seale the daye and yeare first above written — William Bartholomew — Read sealed and delivered in the presence of us — Will : Nebbs — Ric : Tidmvish — Willm Peddington

Probatum fuit Testamentum Suprascriptum apud London coram venerabili et Egregio viro Dno Henrico Marten milite legum Doctore Curiœ Prærogativæ Cant Magro custode sive Comissario ltime constituto vicesimo secundo die menss Julij Anno Dni Millimo sexcenmo Tricesimo quarto Juramento Johannes Bartholomew filij dicti defuncti et Executoris in huiusmodi Testamento nominati Cui comissa fuit Administratio bonorum iurium et creditorum dicti defuncti de bene et fidelr administrando eadem Ad Sancta Dei Evangelia Coram Magistris Christaphoro Glynn et Richo Goddard Clicis vigore Comissionis in ea pte alias emanate Jurat. 66 *Seger.*

Children named in his and his son Richard's wills were

1 Mary[Eng. 4], m. at St. Giles Church, Oxford, Eng., 28 June, 1620, Richard Tidmarsh of Brodwell. She received by her father's will, only a ring; but he bequests to each of her six children, viz.: 1 Merryall, 2 Katherine, 3 John, 4 Ann, 5 Richard and 6 Isabell Tidmarsh.

ii John, as eldest son inherited his father's estate and was the executor of his will. He continued his father's mercantile business in Burford until his death, dying in B., intestate 15 Nov., 1639. It may be* to his memory that the stone near entrance to Bartholomew Chapel is inscribed "Hic Jacet quic quid mortale est Johannis Bartholomew." He had daughter Ann who was buried in B., 16 July, 1637.

2 iii William, b. 1602–3; d. 18 Jan., 1680–1, in Charlestown, Mass.

3 iv Henry, b. 1606–7; d. 22 Nov., 1692, in Salem, Mass.

4 v Richard, b. ab. 1610; is supposed to have died in London or on a return trip from London to Mass.

vi Francis, bapt. in B., 13 Feb., 1613–4; received a bequest by his father's will, but probably died before 1645, as he is not mentioned in the will of his brother Richard.

vii Thomas, bapt. in B., 30 June, 1616; is mentioned in both his father's and brother Richard's wills.

viii Abraham, is mentioned in both of said wills, but died in B., 22 Mar., 1646–7.

ix Sarah, bapt. in B., 14 Apr., 1623; is also mentioned in both wills. A Sarah Bartholomew was m. in B., 13 Apr., 1645, to Thomas Jurden of B. She probably died before 8 Jan., 1658–9, when he married, in B., Margery Hicks.

---

* We naturally wonder who was the originator of Bartholomew Chapel as such. Mr. Henry F. Waters is of the opinion that the portion of St. John's Church so designated was built at the same time as the main church and centuries before the times of these members of the family.

The Bartholomew family may not have been connected in any way with the erection of the church or chapel, but, probably about this time, by their liberality to it and prominence in the church, they were considered entitled to use a portion of it as a family sepulchre and through its use as such this portion obtained its present name.

It has been used as a burial or memorial chapel by our family exclusively and no other family would even now be permitted to place a monument in it.

As there are but three tombs, we naturally apply them to the three brothers who died there, viz.: John in 1643, Richard in 1632 and William in 1634. As the chapel is not mentioned by said William in his will when he gives permission to the overseers of his estate to inter his remains in the Burford Church, it indicates that such a family connection with the church was then probably commenced but had not become sufficiently determined as to be considered an established custom, as he would have considered it if a tomb had already been erected for him. But they were placed there before the overthrow by Cromwell, or before 1645, when the soldiers are said to have torn the inscribed brass plates from them.

And, as John Bartholomew, during that time, was perhaps the most prominent Bartholomew in Burford, and as his name on the portal stone would indicate a prominent part in the establishment of the Chapel, it is not improbable that he was largely instrumental in its establishment. Another fact that encourages this conclusion is that this provides a monument for all heads of families who are known to have died there.

William Bartholomew, known as William the elder, held some positions of esteem in Burford. Those positions did cost him at one point because the town as a whole was not registered with the crown. Because of this, William Bartholomew, the elder, as well as other city officials were charged with crimes.

Named in the criminal offenses were William Taylor, William Bartholomew, Simon Simons, Leonard mills, Thomas Sylvester and john hunt. The rest of the town was charged as well but not named individually. The charge was for exercising without warrant or royal grant the following liberties, privileges and franchises:

holding a weekly market on Saturday;

the holding of annual fairs such as the feast of St. John the Baptist and the feast of Holyrood Day;

the taking of picage and stallage at the market and fairs and exercising of other jurisdictions therein;

the levying of toll on goods exposed for sale and on all livestock brought for sale and the converting toll to the use of the defendants;

the right to felon' goods and chattels;

the right to waifs and strays;

the right to appoint a seneschal of the town;

the right to appoint a deputy alderman;

the right to remove officials from their offices;
the right to hold a borough court every three weeks, and convert to the use of the defendants all profits to the court;
the right to try in that court all cases involving the sum or less than 40s, to administer oaths in hearing of cases and to examine witnesses on oath;
the right to make statutes and by-laws and to fine or imprison persons for breaches thereof; the right to put persons on oath to keep the by-laws.

These rights were revoked but later reinstated. The town went through the proper protocol to gain this rights back.[39]

William Bartholomew was listed as an alderman after the rights were reinstated to Burford. He's listed in 1620 as William Bartholomew the elder. Right before this he had been listed as a town bailiff as well. This one of a few places where he is indicated as William the elder. In his will, above, he's also listed as William the elder. It was a common distinction in Burford for him to be identified this way. It was not clear in the will so much, but it is clear in the town records of alderman due to the fact that his son, William, is listed as an alderman on two separate occasions, before he

---

[39] Gretton, R.H. MA, MBE. *The Burford Records; a Study in Minor Town Government* Oxford University Press, England, 1920 p. 55

came to the Americas. In both of those instances, he is regarded as William Bartholomew Sr.[40] there is some question by George wells Bartholomew and some other Bartholomew historians that there was no proof of William the elder and William of Ipswich of being related due to the fact that William sr. is not listed in the elder's will. But the Burford records make a distinction between the two indicates they were father and son. There may have been other reasons but it would seem there would be another way to distinguish between the two, like William Bartholomew on Drury Street versus Main Street[41]

There are two possibilities as to why this would be the case. One possibility is that William the elder was a devout Anglican and we know this to be true. William senior had become a puritan there is a possibility the two had a falling out. The reason against this would be that William the elder still calls himself William the elder in the will. Why make a distinction at all if you are at odds with someone?

The other possibility is the fact that William the elder died in may of 1634 and had written his will slightly before then. William senior boarded the griffin from London, to Boston in

---

[40] ibid Burford Records p. 98

[41] the street names are for argument sake and not indicative of any known residence.

august of 1634. The possibility is that he announced to the family he was on his way out. It might have occurred to him that the money would have done him no good, especially if the boat sunk for whatever reason and his family who might have been able to use it would have gone without it. William senior was also accomplished by that point and maybe saw no need to take any inheritance whether he stayed or left. With that being said, since he left for the new world in august, and he knew he would move, if he took any possessions, he would have to move them. It would have taken time to move the possessions. They might have been in London[42] for quite some time too, before they secured a ship to the Americas.

Another piece of evidence for William senior being the son of William the elder is that fact that William the elder lists Henry Bartholomew in his will. Henry is also listed in the George Wells Bartholomew book as having migrated to the United States and settled in Salem, Massachusetts. In documentation for the Salem witch trial, which both Henry and William senior were a part of, the two were mentioned as brothers. This solidifies the connections from William

---

[42] A Portrait and Biographical Record of Portage and Summit Counter, A.W. Bowen & Co. Logansport 1808 p.881 this book seems to prove the theory that he had already gone from Burford and would not have been included in his father's will due to his not being present. It seems that he may not have become a Puritan until after he left home so banishment does not seem like the likely reason for his exclusion in his father's will.

senior to William elder as father and son.

Above is pictured the crypt which William Bartholomew the elder was buried in, in St. John the Baptist church in Burford, Oxfordshire, England.

Chapter 4 William Bartholomew Sr. (William Bartholomew of Ipswich)

William Bartholomew of Ipswich was the first to come to the new world. He was born in 1602.

He emigrated from London to Boston in 1634 aboard the ship griffin. Aboard the ship with him was at least a housekeeper listed, as a Bartholomew though likely she was not surnamed Bartholomew. Also on the ship was Ann Hutchison who was a neighbor in Burford and who he testified against in a trial once in Massachusetts.

Included in this chapter, as always, will be pages from George wells Bartholomew. There were also being citations of his involvement in the ann. Hutchison case as well as the Salem witch trial. There will also be included a reprint of the passenger manifesto for the ship griffin as well as many other important documents supporting the history of William Bartholomew of Ipswich.

Here are a few important things to realize about history that lead up to this point.

110 years prior to the birth of William Senior Christopher Columbus crossed the Atlantic in search of the Indies. Eighty-five years prior, Martin Luther nailed Ninety-five Theses to a door. Seventy-five years prior, the bible was translated into the language of the people of Germany.

Three years after the Ninety-five Theses Tyndale posted his own sort of theses. This opened up for the Tyndale New Testament eight years after the German bible. Henry VIII authorized The Great Bible sixty-four years prior. Had Henry VIII not been so bent on a male heir he would not been at odds with the pope. This opened him up to Tyndale and the start of the English reformation and allowed more freedom to reform. Some felt the English reformation didn't go far enough. The persecution against those who wanted to go further caused them to be forced into fleeing for the new world.

WILLIAM BARTHOLOMEW

OF IPSWICH.

2 William[1] (*William*[Eng. 3], *John*[Eng. 2], *John*[Eng. 1],) supposed to be second son* of William and Friswede Bartholomew of Burford, Eng.; was born in 1602 or 3.

He was well educated, undoubtedly a student at the well known "Grammar School"† of Burford, and was probably a fellow student of Peter Heylin, who became chaplain to King Charles I, and afterwards sub-dean of Westminster.

---

*That he was the second son omitted in his father's will (see page 17) appears from the will of his brother Richard (see plate opposite page 53), which mentions him with nearly all his brothers and sisters in the order of their births.

The omission was possibly for the purpose of depriving the second son of his share; for if done because he had already received his part, his father would not, as he did, have studiously avoided mentioning him, and also have excluded him from his portion of the share of any brother or sister who might die childless, and would probably have made William instead of Henry,his heir, in case of John, the eldest son's death, without issue.

If that surmise is correct he was probably disowned on account of his religious faith, as his associations and subsequent opinions show him to have been a "dissenter."

His intimate acquaintance with the noted Mrs. Anne Hutchinson (see his evidence page 31), his accompanying the Rev. John Lothrop and congregation to America, his association with Governor John Leverett as agents of Major Bourne; but more than above, his active and earnest part in the General Court of the colony are conclusive evidence of his puritanism.

Sectarian feeling at that time was extremely bitter. The slightest opposition to the Established Church of England met with terrible chastisement. Heresy ranked worse than treason. It was common for fathers to disown their sons who adopted the new faith, as such prominent examples as the father of Milton, the poet, and Wm. Penn, illustrate.

It is possible that Wm. Bartholomew was a member of the Presbyterian congregation in London, and imprisoned with them; that would have been an abundant reason for disowning him in his sanguine father's loyal mind.

†This school continued in existence for some 200 years.

Isaac Johnson (whose daughter Mary subsequently married W^{m2} Bartholomew(6), Thos. Scott, Mr Wm Hutchinson, Richd Hutchinson, Fr. Hutchinson, Rob't Parker and Tho: Stanley.

1634–5, Mar. 4. "Mr Wm Bartholomewe" and several others were granted privilege to trade (at Ipswich) with visiting vessels.

1635, Apr. 25. Granted several tracts of land in Ipswich.

HOME OF WILLIAM BARTHOLOMEW, IPSWICH, MASS.*

The left L was added about one hundred years ago. The projection on the right hides the front door and the window over the same.

1635, May 6. "Mr Wm Bartholomewe" appeared at the General Court at Boston, as the chosen representative of the inhabitants of Ipswich; he had then only been in America seven months.

This was the first opportunity that the citizens of Ipswich had of showing their appreciation of his settling among them; and the fact that they were exercising that great birthright of Americans, the elective franchise, for about the first time in the history of the world, the honor

* Fell down about 1874. Adjoined present residence of Mrs. Wm. Lord.

of being their choice is apparent. The citizens of Ipswich were some of the best in the colony, including Gov. Thos. Dudley, Major Daniel Dennison (subsequently the highest military officer in the colony), Samuel Appleton, etc., and Wm. Bartholomew's prominence among so many older able men is evidence of his superior education, family and ability.

1635. Was appointed by the General Court with Mr. Dunn to "sett out" the land at Newbury for keeping sheep that came in the Dutch ships.

1635, Sept. 1. The General Court "ordered that Mary ——— servant to Mr. Bartholmewe shall be whipt for runing from her mast^r and shall serve him 6 weeks after her time is ended."

1635, Sept. 2. "Mr Willm Bartholmewe" was again returned to another session of the General Court, in company with Michael Easton who was afterwards governor of Rhode Island five years.

1635–6, Mar. 3. Elected deputy again.

1636, Sept. 8. Wm Pynchon reports to the General Court in delivery of arms, etc., "To Ipswich 8 swords by Mr Wm Bartholomew on the 7th of August 1635."

1637, Sept. 19. He was appointed on a special grand jury in Boston.

At this session the trial of Mrs. Anne Hutchinson came up, in which William Bartholomew took a prominent part. The following is an extract from an order of the court, showing the charge against her. "Whereas the opinions and revelations of Mr. Wheelwright and Mrs. Hutchinson have seduced & led into dangerous errours many of the people here in New England insomuch as there is just cause of suspicion that they, as others in Germany in former times, may upon some revelation make some sudden irruption upon those that differ from them in judgment; for prevention whereof" etc.

His evidence in this case was as follows, viz.:

"I would remember one word to Mrs. Hutchinson among many others. She knowing that I did know her opinions, being she was at my house at London, she was afraid I concieve or loth to impart herself unto me, but when she came within sight of Boston and looking upon the meanness of the place I conceive she uttered these words. If she had not a sure word that England should be destroyed her heart would shake. Now it seemed to me at that time very strange that she should say so."

Mrs. H. remarked. "I do not remember that I looked upon the meanness of the place nor did it discourage me, because I knew the bounds of my habitation were determined" etc.

Mr. Bartholomew continued: "I speak as a member of the court, I fear that her revelations will deceave."

Governor Sir Henry Vane. "Have you heard any of her revelations?"

Mr. Bartholomew. "For my own part I am very sorry to see her now here and I have nothing against her but what I said was to discover what manner of spirit Mrs. Hutchinson is of; only as I remember as we were once going through Pauls church yard* she then was very inquisitive after revelations and said that she had never had any great thing done about her but it was revealed to her beforehand."

Mrs. Hutchinson. "I say the same thing again."

Mr. Bartholomew. "And also that she said she was come to New England but for Mr. Cottons sake. As for Mr. Hooker (as I remember) she said she liked not his spirit, only she spake of a sermon of his in the Low Countries where in he said this—it was revealed to me yesterday that England should be destroyed.

She took notice of that passage and it was very accept-

---

* A street in London, Eng.

able with her. (This passage is in print and Mr. Hooker avowed it afterwards at Hartford.)

Mr. Cotton (Teacher of Boston Church). "One thing let me intreat you to remember, Mr. Bartholomew, you never spoke anything to me."

"Mr. Bartholomew. No, sir. I never spake of it to you and therefore I desire to clear Mr. Cotton."

Gov. "There needs no more of that."

Mr. Bartholomew. "Only I remember her eldest daughter said in the ship that she had a revelation that a young man in the ship should be saved, but he must walk in the ways of her mother."

1637, Nov. 2. He was returned as deputy from Ipswich this and the following sessions.

1639. Was chosen to convey the instructions of the General Court to Captains Wiggins and Chapupenoon, etc., at Piscataque.

1639, June. "Mr. Will Bartholomew granted fourty shillings for his journey to Piscataque."

1639, July 22. "Mr. Bartholomew offered to entertain Mrs. Jupe (teacher of the Ipswich School) freely for a year without charge, if she have health, but if she prove sick, the charge to be borne by the publicke."

He was granted by the town of Ipswich eighty acres, of land, in consideration of charges in going to courts, lying near Mr. Hubbard's farm.

Was town clerk of Ipswich. Fees for same were the "3[d] of fines for not attending meetings" (of the Established or Congregational Church).

This is a striking illustration of the strong religious and sectarian character of the inhabitants.

1641, Oct. 7. Again deputy for Ipswich.

1641, Dec. 10. "Mr. Bartholomew" appointed with two others by the General Court to place valuation on certain property.

1642, Apr. 6. It was voted by the town of Ipswich:

"The Town doth trust Mr. Bartholomew to copy the old Waste Book, and such other papers as the Recorder shall commit unto him, and he shall be paid for his paynes." The copy made in accordance with this vote is the oldest record possessed by the town. It is in his handwriting, and is a very good specimen of the chirography of the age. The following is a fac-simile.

TRANSLATION OF THE ABOVE.

"granted to William Barthollmew one acre in the high street Robert Lordes house lott east and Edward Brownes house lott west: also eighty acres of land in consideration of charges in going to courtes: lying neare Mr Hubbards ffarme W B"

1645, May 14. Appointed on a Committee to report on best manner of destroying "Ye wolves, wch are such ravenous cruel creatures & daily vexatious to all ye inhabitants of ye collony."

1646. Chosen by the town to lay out way to John Caldwells house.

Was one of the chosen "seven men" of the town.

1647, May 26. "Mr. Wm Bartholomew" deputy.

1647. Major Daniel Dennison presented himself as deputy in place of Mr. Bartholomew for Ipswich; but on information that all ye freeman had not notice of the election he was not accepted.

1648. He was one of the largest subscribers to a yearly compensation to Major Daniel Dennison "to encourage him in his military helpfulness" as their leader.

1649. Chosen one of the "Seven men" of Ipswich; also to lay out highways; also allowed compensation for his expense in a journey to Salem about the vote.

1650. Deputy while brother Henry was same for Salem.

1650, Jan. 11. Appointed with Major Daniel Dennison to assist the Messrs. Payne, benefactors of the town of Ipswich, in establishing a public school and taking charge of same. He was made feoffee of the school and continued to act in those capacities as long as he remained in Ipswich. The school is still in existence, and still recognizes the necessity of complying with the conditions of the benefaction.

1650, June 21. Again appears as deputy for term commencing that date.

Copy of an act of that term of the courte.

"Whereas M^r^. Wm Bartholmew of Ipswich and M^r^. Henry Bartholmew of Salem have tendered themselves to supply fifty shillings apiece in money towards the chardge of our commissioners of the Collonies, itt is ordered by this courte, that Mr. W^m^ & Mr Henry Bartholmew shall be pajd the same out of the next country role in each towne of the best pay with allowance of six pence upon every five shillings for forbearance and other inconveniences, unless it be paid in money in November next."

The colony felt too poor to continue the Commissioners' Court; the latter was an important step towards our federated form of government and the precursor of our present congress.

The great wisdom shown by William and Henry Bartholomew in this generous personal effort to continue the federal union of the colonies is, in light of succeeding history, seemingly prophetic.

Oct. 2. Records show he bargained for 30,000 hogshead staves.

1651, Jan. 26. Chosen on a committee to establish and regulate a grammar school. " Shall allso consider the best way to make provision for teaching to write and cast account."

1653. Sells several tracts of land in Ipswich and Topsfield, the deeds to which his wife, Ann, signs with a mark.

1654, June 28. Chosen treasurer of the county.

Appointed by the General Court " to divide ye Colonies arms among ye shires."

1654–5, Mar. 2. Re-conveyed to town of Ipswich, for the nominal consideration of five pounds the entire tract granted him in 1639 ; and the town divided this and other tracts among its citizens as a common pasture, which has ever since been known as "Bartholomew Hill Pasture,"* and so mentioned in the town records as early as 1656 ; thus preserving the name of the town's early citizen and friend to its later inhabitants in a most pleasant manner.

1655, May 23. Appointed with two others to go to Squamscott and make a just division under petition of Mr. Thos. Lake. Report signed W^{m}. Bartholomew.

Was a commissioner.

June 20. "Mr. W^{m}. Bartholomew, Mr. Sam Maverick" and others, gave bond for £2,300 (about equal to the present value of $50,000) for appearance of Mr. John Gifford.

---

* Bartholomew Hill Pasture is situated two miles west of the centre of Ipswich village, and contains nearly a square mile. It is covered with excellent grass, and has a single row of willow trees through its centre, crossing the tops of the peaks of its double hill. The heights of these peaks are 201 and 204 feet.

This pasture is divided into numerous " cow rights," each of which represents about two acres, and is held in common by the owners. These " cow rights " are conveyed and inherited as real estate, but never in modern times subdivided or partitioned.

Major Nehemiah Bourne of London, who had been a major in Rainsborough's regiment in Cromwell's overthrow of Charles I, appointed John Leverett and William Bartholomew his agents in Boston.

Mr. Leverett was one of the grand men of Massachusetts' colonial history, representative, speaker, major general, assistant, deputy governor and governor many years, agent of the colony in England, etc. "No man," says Savage, "in our country, ever filled more important offices, nor with happier repute."

Mr. Bartholomew's association with Governor Leverett, by Major Bourne, who knew both well, having lived in Boston, is proof, if such were wanting, that William Bartholomew was both a business-like and honorable man.

Copy of power of attorney: "Know all men by these p^rnts y^t I Nehemiah Bourne of London Esqr for diuers good causes & consideracons me hereunto mouing haue made &c, my Loueing friends Jno Leverett of Boston, merchant & Wm Bartholmew of Ipswich m^rchant my true & Lawfull Atturneys in New England.

March 26 1655. Nehe: Bourne
& a Seale.

In p^rence of
ffra Mosse not pub.
Hen Mosse not pub.
Jere: Jeneway Peter Tilly.

Recorded Nov. 30 1655 at Request of M^r W^m. Bartholomew."

1655, Nov. 13. Appointed with two others by the General Court to settle certain troubles and divisions between the towns.

1656, May 22. "Mr Willjam Bartholomew" appointed with Major Wm Hawthorn and Mr. Sam'l Hall to treat with the inhabitants of Hamden and Strawbery Bancke etc., and to conclude what they judge meet between the towns and persons.

1656, Oct. 14. Appointed to assist in laying out 1,000 acres of land for Mr William Hubbard, Sen., of Ipswich.

1657, May 6. "Mr Wm Bartholomew" (the "M^r" is mentioned so often, because it indicated the social position he held. Ministers, military officers and those of superior standing in the community were called Mr., but the most of the deputies of the General Court, the highest body in the colony, were plain John, etc.) appointed a commissioner to settle troubles concerning boundaries of Salisbury and Hampton.

1658. Still owner of his High street lot in Ipswich.

1659, July 21. W^m. Bartholomew, of Ipswich, merchant, purchases of Robert Nash, and wife Sarah, house and lot in Boston, bounded as follows: west by Joseph Peck, east by W^m. Franklin, southwest by W^m. Makepiece and northeast by Mill Creek.

This is the last mention of him as of Ipswich, and the date of filing the above for record in Boston, 15 March, 1660, probably is about the date of his removal to Boston, as he is mentioned there within a year after as a merchant, and as living on the above described property.

1662, May 1. Appointed overseer of mill of W^m. Brown of Boston.

Have not been able to learn the relationship, if any, existing between Wm Brown of Boston and Edward Brown of Ipswich who called W^m. Bartholomew "brother."

It was probably at this time that W^m. Bartholomew, Jr., learned the mill business.

1665, May 3. His name heads a petition of fourteen prominent citizens of Boston, requesting that the commissioners see that the estate of Samuel Maverick, Junior, of Boston, be properly settled.

1665, Nov. 4. Appointed to assist in inventoring Samuel Maverick Junr's Estate.

1666. Treasurer of County.

1666, May 23. Appointed with two others to provide relief for some 250 French from St. Christopher's, at public charge; authorizing them to make contracts with masters of ships for their transportation at the expense of the colony.

1667. He assisted in drawing Elizabeth Robinson's will, and in after litigation he testified as follows: "That the said Elizabeth came often to the house of this deponant diuers times weeping to him, to get her will formerly drawne to be altered & to be new drawne. My business being more than ordinary, I could not in some weekes attend it, but some time before the date of her last will, went to M[r] Wiswall at her request, and wee together tooke this her last will from her owne mouth wording it as meetly as we might, but in nothing altering the sence of her mind expressed to vs.

I doe not remember wee dictated, anything to her of it, but only when she was speaking of some bequeathed to her kindred in England wee wished her to insert that clause, viz[t]. if the estate might afford; & whereas she had drawne two formes of wills before, I doe account this will the most rationall of them all, & the Reasons she gave for altering her former will, were upon rationall grounds, & I doe affirme to my best vnderstanding, that at the drawing & at the signing & sealing of this her last will & Testament she was of a composed & deposing mind. Also she declared herself severall times to this deponant, after the will was signed & finished, to be well sattisfyed & quieted in her mind, w[ch] indeed seemed restless until it was done; further this deponant testifyeth, that hee said deponant meeting her the Euening before she sickened, going from her House, it being a very cold Euening, asked her why shee would hazard her health soe, as to goe forth in soe cold an Euening, she answered mee, that she was going to a priuate meeting. And to my best remembrance I then asked her as I had done vpon occation at times before, whether shee heard with vnderstanding at the meetings & shee said Yea, shee praysed God for it. Taken vpon oath the 29 of the 7 : 1667."

1668, Sept. 1. "Edmund Gibbon, now in Boston, haue appointed M[r] Humfry Hodges & M[r] Willm Barthomew, merch[ts] my true and lawful attornies."

He was frequently called upon to make and witness wills, inventory estates, oversee estates and persons, made feoffee of property in trust, etc.

In 1668 he is mentioned in connection with Mr. Humfry Hodges as merchants, and in 1677 in same connection with Joshua Atwater; they may have been his partners.

1679, Nov. 25. With his wife Ann, he makes a deed to his nephew Henry Bartholomew of all his property real and personal. It is a peculiar deed and there was probably some urgent reason for making it that is unexplained.

"Mr William Bartholomew late of Boston, now sojourning with Mr Green in Charlestoune deceased this life 18th day of Januar[y] 1680" (1681, new style). (From Charlestown records.)

No will is found; he probably made none as he had apparently divided his property among his children before his death. The inventory of his remaining estate is as follows:

Charlestowne 17th 4. 1681

An Inventory of an Estate of William Bartholomew Deceased taken and Estimated by us whose names are subscribed

	lb. s. d.
Imprimis To one ffeatherbed & bolsters & 1 pillow two Ruggs & paire of Blankets, & old shattred bedsted . . .	04-00-00
It Old Andirons Tonges, fire shovle & spitt & pot hooks &c.	00-12-00
To old chaires, joint stooles, Cushions & paire of old bellows	00-08-06
To ½ doz[n] Cushions	00-06-00

To brasse: vizt: 2 old Kettles with 2 trivets	1–0–0		
It other small brasse things	0–9–0	1–16–0	01–16–00
It old brasse things	0–7–0		
To one doz^{n} Napkins & Tablecloth			00–11–00
To 2 Cuppboard Cloths			00–04–00
To old sheets 3 paire spaire Course pillow cases 1 course shirt and nine old Course Towells			00–18–06
To 4 doz$^{n.}$ Childrens stiff Capps			00–03–00
A small Remn^{t} of Cotton Cloth, & of speckled Linnen & of home made cloth and of Kersie			00–08–00
To old Pewter			00–08–06
To Books viz$^{t.}$ A bible in 2to: Clarks Martyrologie, &c.			00–16–03
To old blanketts worn out wth peices & such like Coverled			00–10–00
To old boxes & Chest and Lumber			00–06–06
To 5 old Table cloths			00–04–00
To an old Trunk 3$^{s.}$ & 3 Chests 2$^{s.}$ 6^{d}			00–05–06
To an old fowling peice, 15$^{s.}$ 1 mach lock musy^{t} & sword 8^{s}			01–03–00
To two old small Ruggs			00–08–00
To a parcell of Indian Hatchets			00–12–00
To a parcell of hows			02–00–00
To 2 Iron Potts			00–07–06
To a Blew Rugg			00–11–00
To an old Carpett			00–07–00
To two old Hammackers			00–09–00
To Pewter			02–08–00
To Tin small things			00–02–06
To 1 paire of old Sheets			00–06–00
To 8 yd^{s} Canvas 8^{s} To 9 yd^{s} narrow Canvas 5^{s} . .			00–13–00
To two Earthen Juggs			00–02–06
To 1 Cutlesse 5$^{s.}$ an old brass Kettle 5^{s}			00–10–00
		21–17–3	

Mr Jacob Green is
granted Admin to
the estate of m^{r}
w^{m} Bartholomew deced
& took oath to y^{e} Inventory

Estimated by us.
Samuel Phipps
Nicholas Meade

His grave in Phipps Street Cemetery, Charlestown, is in a prominent position adjoining that of John Harvard, the benefactor of Harvard College; the inscription on the gravestone reads "William Bartholmew ag^{d} 78 y^{rs} dec^{d} Jan^{ry} 18th 1680."

William Bartholomew was of good parentage. He enjoyed unusual educational advantages and probably received a practical business training in his father's store, which, if conformity can be expected with his will, must have been conducted with great care and thoroughness.

Leaving the paternal roof we find him before the age

of thirty-two in London, married, keeping house and probably in some mercantile employment.

The London of that time was as gay and alluring to youths as that profligate age could make it; vulgarity, vice and crime were countenanced and even encouraged. Under these circumstances the young man who chose his company from a persecuted and derided, but devoutly religious sect, showed a strong and noble character.

Surrounded by oppression, and perhaps disowned by his father, it is not strange that such a spirit should wish to breathe a freer air, should brave the dreaded ocean and join the Puritan settlers in the wilds of America.

The facts given show the high standard he maintained in his adopted home. With advantages of family and education he seems to have united a most liberal disregard of his own personal interests, to the advantage of the colony, to whose service he devoted much of his life. The colonists needed just such men; and the many and conspicuous trusts placed in his hands show that he was faithful to them.

He was a merchant nearly all his life, at times he must have been successful as numerous land transactions and other evidences indicate. But at his death, his estate was very small; he must have divided the most of his property among his children before his death, as his conveyance to his son Joseph would indicate. He died at the home of his only daughter. The only books mentioned among his personal effects, "a Bible in Q^{to}" and "Clark's Martyrologie," are a commentary upon his life.

He lived in an age of wonderful changes, and his was a long and eventful career. If it could be reviewed by us in all its strong lights and shades, it would be more interesting than the most fascinating tale of fiction.

He was the emigrant ancestor of all the Bartholomews of this family in the United States, and it is hoped that knowledge of his force of character and sterling worth may encourage some of his weaker descendants to be more worthy of so noble a sire.

Mrs. Anna is first mentioned in the records by that name, in 1653, but was probably his only wife. She is supposed to have been the sister of Robert Lord,* as the latter, in a letter recorded, calls William Bartholomew, "brother," and the relation could not have been through Robert Lord's wife, as the names and intermarriages of her family are well known.

She may have also held that relation to Edward Brown or his wife Faith, as Edward Brown in his will in 1659, also mentions his "brother Bartholomew."

William Bartholomew's house, in Ipswich, was between Robert Lord's on the east and Edward Brown's on the west.

She survived her husband and died in Charlestown, 29 Jan., 1682–3. Her gravestone, still standing in Charlestown, is inscribed A. B. died Jan., 1682–3. Children:

i Mary, m., first, by Major Daniel Dennison, in Gloucester, 24 Dec., 1652 (Salem records say 1657), Mathew, son of Mathew Whipple† of Ipswich, who died 20 Oct., 1657. She m. 2nd, as his second wife, Jacob, son of Elder John Greene‡ of Charlestown. By his first wife Elizabeth (Long) he had children, Jacob, b. 11 Oct., 1654; Joseph, who d. 26 Aug., 1657 and John. He was of the artillery company, 1650, freeman 1650, representative 1677 and town clerk of C. In 1667 Mary, joined by her husband, made her father her attorney to settle with John Whipple her right to property left her by her former husband. This power was not recorded until 1676. Her children were:

1 Mathew Whipple, b. 20 Dec., 1657; posthumous.

* Robert Lord married, about 1630, Mary, dau. of Sam'l and Mary (Ward) Waite of Wethersfield, Essex. Eng. He emigrated from London to Ipswich, in 1634. Was for many years town clerk, etc., of Ipswich.

† Mathew Whipple, Ipswich, Mass., had grant of land 1638, d. 1647, leaving eldest son John[2], born, no doubt, in England, wid[e] Rose, who was his second wife and children, Mary, *Mathew*, Ann, Elizabeth and Joseph born about 1646, whose order of succession is not known." (Savage.)

‡ "John Greene came in the James from London, 1632, arrived 12 June, with w. Perseverance & 3 chn.: John, *Jacob*, Abigail, Sarah Jones a servant & Joseph,

2 Elizabeth Greene, b. ab. 1661; d. 7 Apr., 1679, æt. 17 (gravestone).
3 Mary Greene, b. 13 May, 1662; d. 20 Aug., 1666, æt. 4 (gravestone).
4 Bartholomew Greene, b. Mar., 1663–4; bap. Feb., 1664–5.
5 Dorcas Greene, bap. 31 Dec., 1665; m. 1681, John Brackenburg.
6 Joseph Greene, b. Apr., 1668; d. May, 1684, æt. 16.

5 ii Joseph, b. about 1638; resided in London, Eng., in 1693.
6 iii William, b. in 1640–1; d. in spring of 1697.

In the footnotes, George Wells Bartholomew mentions, William Senior came over with a Reverend John Lothrop. It is important to discuss him to bring deeper understanding to the Bartholomew heritage and what life looked like at the time.

A quick note of interest for John Lothrop was that his descendants around the world, per his Wikipedia article number over 80,000. These include six presidents of the United States, the founder of Stanford, early leaders in the Mormon Church as well as many well-known celebrities.[43]

He is also said to be the one who coined the concept,

[43] https://en.wikipedia.org/wiki/John_Lothropp#cite_note-4

separation of church and state, or religious freedom, which was not popular in England got him arrested. No known records attribute the phrasing to him but the concept was evident.[44]

The next piece gives a little insight into what was going on at the time as it relates to William Senior's pastor and congregation. It is an excerpt from an extract in the Roxbury Records. The extract is of Governor Winthrop's Journal dated Sept. 18, 1634.

"The *Griffin* and another ship now arriving with about 200 passengers and one hundred cattle, Mr. Lathrop and Mr. Sims, two godly ministers, coming in the same ship."

"Mr. Lothrop was the first regularly settled minister of the First Parish in Scituate, consisting of sixty-three members. He took charge of it Jan. 18, 1634-5. He removed to Barnstable with twenty heads of families five years later, Oct. 11, 1639. Among these faithful adherents were Anthony Annable, James Cudworth and Henry Ewell.

In 1616 Mr. Henry Jacob established the first Congregational Church in England, at London, on the plan of Mr. Robinson's at Leyden, he having consulted with him on

[44] ibid

the subject. Mr. Jacob having removed to Virginia in 1624, Mr. Lathrop became his successor in London. The church held their meetings privately, and escaped the vigilance of their persecutors until April 29, 1632, when they were discovered by Tomlinson, the pursuivant of the Bishop, holding a meeting for religious worship at the house of Mr. Humphrey Barnet in Blackfriars. Forty-two of them were apprehended, and eighteen only escaped.

Mr. Lothrop with others was imprisoned, where he remained until April, 1634 - two full years; and was then set at liberty on condition of departing from the kingdom. He embarked in the ship *Griffin* for Boston with about thirty of his church and people, and arrived Sept. 18, 1634."[45]

Of the two ships Governor Winthrop noted, William Bartholomew was on the Ship Griffin. It does not list any children or his wife so it is possible the other ship contained his family. The other ship is not known. The person listed as Mrs. Bartholomew on the Griffin is not William's wife. William's wife who immigrated with him is Anna Bartholomew. Her maiden name was Lord.

45

http://www.anamericanfamilyhistory.com/Lothrop%20Family/LothropJohn1584.html

The passenger list for the 1634 Atlantic trip of the Ship Griffin is as follows:

Bartholomew, William

Bartholomew, Mrs. Mary

Haines, William

Haines, Richard

Heaton, Nathaniel

Heaton, Mrs. Elizabeth

Heaton, Samuel

Heaton, Jabez

Heaton, Leah

Heaton, Mary

Hutchinson, William

Hutchinson, Mrs. Anne

Hutchinson, Edward

Hutchinson, Faith

Hutchinson, Bridget

Hutchinson, William

Hutchinson, Samuel

Hutchinson, Mary

Hutchinson, Ann

Hutchinson, Susanna

Lothrop, John

Lothrop, Mrs. (wife)

Lothrop, Thomas

Lothrop, Samuel

Lothrop, Joseph

Lothrop, John

Lothrop, Benjamin

Lothrop, Jane

Lothrop, Barbara

Lynde, Thomas

Lynde, Mrs. Margeret

Lynde, Thomas

Lynde, Henry

Symmes, Rev. Zachariah

Symmes, Mrs. Sarah

Symmes, William

Symmes, Mary

Symmes, Elizabeth

Symmes, Huldah

Symmes, Hannah

Symmes, Rebecca

Other sources include:

Cotton, Rev. John

Haynes, John

Mygatt, Joseph

Hammond, Benjamin

Hammond, Elizabeth (Widow)

Hammond, Elisabeth

Hammond, Martha

Hammond, RachelHammond, Benjamin[46]

According to the same source, one other ship sailed into Boston. Other sources have other ships, but their landing dates were different. The other sources do not indicate if the others were Pilgrim ships or not. The other ship into Boston does not have a landing date or an available passenger list. It was called the Ship Regard.[47] It could be, the Regard had cattle in it, but as Governor Winthrop accounted for, there were two hundred passengers, and even with the extras from other sources, there aren't two hundred on the Griffin. William of Ipswich's (also William Senior) wife and children also migrated at the same time, so whether it be the Regard or the other ship they were likely on the other ship.

As far as the other two reverends on the Griffin according to this list, both are well documented in other works and will not be included here. This will also be true of Governor Winthrop whose statement about the ships was recorded earlier.

---

[46] http://www.packrat-pro.com/ships/griffin.htm Other sources have Rev. Cotton on the Griffin a year earlier in July however, it is only known otherwise that the Griffin's first voyage to the America's was in 1634 and had one other subsequent voyage.

[47] http://www.packrat-pro.com/ships/shiplist.htm

A quick insight on the time frame of the Griffin was the fact that it was fourteen years after the Mayflower landed at Plymouth Rock.

Once off the ship England, William Senior settled quickly in Ipswich. It did not take William a long time to become active in the public servant scene in Ipswich. He represented citizens in the Boston general court and held many public offices. In 1670 he moved to Boston as a commerce mogul and held many public servant positions in Boston, which included head of the treasury for the colony.[48] The Boston general served as an executive branch, a legislative branch and a judicial branch in Colonial Massachusetts.[49] William also served and represented trade agreements. This may have been a part of his public servant position or in part because of his public service.[50]

In 1647, William Bartholomew was elected as a deputy in the House of Deputies.[51] The House of Deputies was later changed to the House of Representatives.[52] In 1650, he was

---

[48] ibid A Portrait and Biography

[49] http://www.encyclopedia.com/history/dictionaries-thesauruses-pictures-and-press-releases/general-court-colonial

[50] https://ipswichwades.wordpress.com/tag/massachusetts-bay-colony/

[51] Records of Massachusetts Vol. III 1644-1657 p.

[52] http://www.encyclopedia.com/history/dictionaries-thesauruses-pictures-

once again returned to his position as Deputy representing the people of Ipswich[53] and in 1660; William retained the title of Deputy. Both he and his brother Henry were paid by the colony in advance for their services.[54] In 1655 William was part of a commission who went to Squamscot and assisted with a land division.[55] The earliest known date for William to have served in the House of Deputies was 1637[56]. It seems by research, the term was three years. Because he disembarked the Ship Griffin in 1634 during the first year of a term he would not have had the opportunity to serve. But the first chance he could, he was in the House of Deputies. George Wells Bartholomew does have him serving as early as 1635 as returned to the House. To return to the house implies the possibility that he served as representative quickly. He'd been granted a freeman earlier in 1635 per George Wells and that gave him permission to own land, be

---

and-press-releases/general-court-colonial

[53] Records of the Governor and Company of the Colony of Massachusetts Bay in New England Vol. IV Part I 1650-1660 printed by the order of Legislature p. 2

[54] ibid p. 202

[55] Ibid 394 He was also mentioned on p411 in relation to a commission dealing with land

[56] Records of the Governor and Company of the Colony of Massachusetts Bay in New England Vol. I Part I 1628-1641 printed by the order of Legislature p. 220

a member of the church and also serve in the House of Deputies.

One of the biggest things William Bartholomew did in his first year as Deputy was testify against Anne Hutchinson in the General Court in Boston. George Wells Bartholomew covers pieces of the trial including William's testimony against her. The charges brought against her were of antinomianism, which were also brought against Rev. Cotton. Cotton was cleared of any charges of heretical teaching. Because he was cleared, she was subsequently excommunicated and banished due to slander against the clergy. [57] The Scarlet Letter mentions Anne Hutchinson and some of her case may be the inspiration for the writing.

William Bartholomew is listed as a witness in the Salem Witch Trials.[58] A quote was given to his witness,

"We present John Bradstreet, of Rowley, for suspicion of having familiarity with the Devil. He said he read in a book of magic, and that he heard a voice asking him what work he had for him. He answer, 'Go make a bridge of sand over the sea; go make a ladder of sand up to heaven, and go to God, and come down no more.'

---

[57] http://www.history.com/topics/anne-hutchinson

[58] Upham, Charles *Salem Witchcraft* Dover Publications Mineola 2000 p not numbered

"Witness hereof, Francis Parat and his wife of Rowley"

"Witness, William Bartholomew, of Ipswich"

Rowley was not found guilty of Witchcraft. However he was found guilty of lying. This was his second conviction of lying and he was sentenced to pay twenty shilling or be whipped. The final determination was that he had fantasticized the whole event.[59]

A nine and eleven year old girl were the original accusers of the Salem Witches. Those who spoke out against them, they accused them of being witches as well.[60] Nearly two hundred in all were accused. Twenty were hung and one was tortured or pressed to death. Some died in jail awaiting trial. Some died in prison after the conviction.[61]

The Salem Witch Trials were bogus for the fact that they used the case law written about in "The Tryal of Witches" in England where spectral evidence was allowed in the courtroom[62]

---

[59] ibid p428

[60] Yost, Melissa http://salem.lib.virginia.edu/people?group.num=&mbio.num=mb33 2002

[61] http://historyofmassachusetts.org/salem-witch-trials-victims/

[62] Harrison, Rick; Romney, Rebecca: *Pawn Stars;* History Channel 2017

William had four children. It is not known if he had more than one wife. His fourth child was born in 1658. Anna Lord would have been fifty-two. It was recorded, she was "near confinement" after the birth of the fourth child. The record doesn't specify why she was near confinement or if she was Anna Lord or if he had a different wife.[63] Nothing prior to Anna's marriage to William is known right away. George Wells among other sources know nothing specifically about her except that her brother moved from England too and was next-door neighbors in Ipswich. When studying her brother, Robert Lord (Lorde) it opens up much more information about Anna. We find her parents and from there are able to trace the Lord family back further than the Bartholomew family. Some branches that married into the Lord family go back to pre Norman invasion and beyond. Prior to that, while heritage is tracked, most are considered legend as the sources are not considered historical but are recorded nonetheless. Her family has much nobility and pre Norman Conquest it shows royalty but royalty at that time was kings over towns or cities similar to nobility rule as far as land possessed. However, as far as rule, they were sole leadership in that kingdom. The kings again are legendary and not necessarily historic at a certain point. As far as

[63] Anderson, Charles, The Great Migration, vol 1, A-B, (New England Historical Genealogical Society, Boston 1999, pps. 180-186

nobility, there does not seem to be a ton of information on the family as there are for others in nobility. Perhaps they stayed out of confrontation with their nobility or royalty.

Anna's father's name was also Robert. They were from Sudbury, Suffolk, England. Robert was christened in January of 1576 at All Saints Church and died in Sudbury.

Most sources have his wife as Katherine Thompson but FindAGrave has her listed as Katherine Bartholomew. Even if her maiden name were Bartholomew, being from Suffolk she is either a distant cousin or not related to our line at all. FindAGrave has Katherine listed as Robert's mother which makes sense and other sources list her as wife to Anthony. The problem sometimes with these studies is spouses may have the same name and the generations get confused. Some sources had Katherine Thompson married to Robert Sr.'s father, Anthony, but those were easily debunked based on ages. It is more probably than not that Katherine is the name of both Anthony and Robert's wives. It's more likely for Thompson to be married to Robert and Bartholomew to be married to Anthony. Some sources have two generations with someone named Anthony and some have Robert Sr. named Robert Anthony Lord.

The theory is that Katherine was born Katherine

Thompson. She has the name Katherine Bartholomew and then Katherine Lord. Katherine Lord was definitely Katherine Thompson at birth and her parents are verified. Katherine Bartholomew could be a married name if she was married once before. The FindAGrave entry shows an entry for a birth but not for a death. Katherine Lord came to Massachusetts Bay Colony as a widow. Katherine Lord's death is recorded and she is known as the widow. That Katherine Lord is known as Katherine Thompson. Some records show Anna was made fun of for marrying a Bartholomew since her mother was known as Katherine Bartholomew. It was like she was marrying family. The fact that we know her brother was Robert Lord and Katherine Lord lived with Faith, one of the other siblings.

All of Anna's male siblings, for a couple generations in the Lord branch were born in Sudbury, Suffolk, England. Sudbury is in the greater London area. She and her entire family including grandparents are said to have immigrated to Massachusetts Bay Colony to Ipswich though for grandparents it would have been before the Mayflower. This is not from any primary sources. Anna's mother immigrated and lived with Anna's sister, Faith, until she died. She was known as Katherine Lord in the records of her death. Anna was one of more than ten children. It is not certain again if Robert had one wife or two but at least for sure Katherine

Thompson.

Anna's family tree as follows includes: father Robert 1576-1635[64] (Katherine Thompson, 1580-1650 and possible Katherine Bartholomew), Anthony 1540-1603 (wife unknown), John Lord 1525-1568 (Elizabeth Robinson 1527-1570) Thomas Lord 1490-1560 (Elspeth Brereton 1489-1515) Harry Lord 1468-1500 (Sioned Bagot 1457-1490) William Lord 1447-1510 (wife unknown).

Anna Lord's relation to Robert can be seen as William refers to Robert as brother and Faith, who is Robert's sister, married Edward Browne. Edward in his will also refers to William as brother. At the time if you said brother in law it has the same blanket meaning as the sibling of your spouse but in canon law it gave the same rights as a brother as a brother in law or a father and father in law. There were no distinctions under the law as to which referred to which. For Edward Brown or Robert Lord referring to him as brother, in law did not need to be added, as it was understood[65].

William Bartholomew died in 1680. He was buried in the Phipps Street Burying Ground, Charleston, and

---

[64] 1635 was the year after the Griffin landed.

[65] https://en.m.wikipedia.org/wiki/Parent-in-law

Massachusetts.

[66]

[66] Picture provided by Dave Bartholomew from his trip out East 12 years ago.

Chapter 5 Lt. William Bartholomew Jr.

Lt. William Bartholomew Junior was in the first generation of Bartholomew's born in the United States. George Wells Bartholomew mentions there is no direct proof of William Junior being the son of William Senior. The case for it is that we know that William senior had a son named William born around the same time. There are not any other known Bartholomew's in the area that would have had children at the time, other than William senior's brother Henry. Henry had a son named William but he was not born until after lt. William Bartholomew. He also could not have been henrys' son because he was a junior. William junior also served in the house of deputies.[67]

The way that things were done in the Massachusetts Bay Colony at the time was called the Winthrop society. In order to be able to hold membership in church, you had to take the oath of the freeman. Once a freeman you could vote or even run for political office and serve in the court. Aside from William and Henry, there were no other Bartholomew's at the time who were freeman. You could not be a freeman

[67] Hitchcock, Frederick, The Register of the Colonial Dames of the State of New York, New York 1913 p 266

except at the discretion of Governor Winthrop.[68]

Lt. William Bartholomew is never on the rolls as having taken the oath of the freeman. it is likely that he was born into freeman status. When he would have served in the general court he still would have had to be a church member and a freeman. If he did not take the oath of the freeman how did he get in the court? Even though nothing specifically says you can be born into as a freeman, everything indicates that would be the case.

The oath of the freeman that his father would have taken is as follows:

I, A&B, being by God's providence an inhabitant and freeman within the jurisdiction of this common wealth, do freely acknowledge myself to be subject to the government thereof, and therefore do hereby swear by the great and dreadful name of the ever-living God that I will be true and faithful to the same, and will accordingly yield assistance and support thereunto, with my person and estate, as in equity I am bound, and will also truly endeavor to maintain and preserve all the privileges and liberties thereunto, submitting myself to the wholesome laws made and established by the same. And further, that I will not plot nor practise any evil against it, nor consent to any that shall be so done, but will timely discover and reveal the same to lawful authority now here established for the speedy preventing thereof. Moreover, I do solemnly bind myself in the sight of God that when

---

[68] http://winthropsociety.com/doc_freemen.php

I shall be called to give my voice touching any such matter of this State, wherein Freemen are to deal, I will give my vote and suffrage as I shall in my own conscience judge best to produce and tend to the public wealth of the body, without respect of persons or respect of any man. So help me God in the Lord Jesus Christ.

6 William[2] (*William*[1],* *William*,) born probably in

William Bartholomew (1688.)

william Bartholomew (1697 to will.)

Ipswich, in 1640–1, married in Roxbury, Mass., 17 Dec., 1663, Mary, daughter of Captain Isaac and Elizabeth (Porter) Johnson, and granddaughter of John Johnson who held the title of "Surveyor of all ye Kings armies in America." Both the grandfather and father represented Roxbury many years in the General Court and held high, social rank. Capt. Isaac Johnson was killed 19 Dec., 1675, in the famous "Narragansett Fort Fight," leading his men over the bridge (a fallen tree) into the Indians fort.

He died in the spring of 1697. Mrs. Mary was born 24 April, 1642, and was living, in 1705, in Branford, Conn.

Lieut. William Bartholomew seems to have early taken a practical view of life as is shown by his learning the carpenters' trade.

In 1662, he probably received his first experience in the mill business, which he afterwards carried on extensively, as his father was that year made overseer of William Brown's mill in Boston; and he may have subsequently

---

* Positive proof that he was son of William Bartholomew, of Ipswich, has not been found, but all evidence obtained favors that conclusion.

(1663) assisted his uncle Henry in building the Old South Mills in Salem.

The last of June, 1663, he was apparently staying about ten miles from Medfield, Mass., and was perhaps engaged as a carpenter or millwright at Robert Heusdale's mill. He there took part in a wolf hunt and with others had some trouble with a party of Indians who wanted liquor which was refused them. His testimony given 5 April, 1664, is as follows:

"John Levin aged twenty ffour yeares or thereabout & William Bartholomew aged twenty three both sworne testiffie & saye that beinge at a ffarme at Mr. Richard Parkers about tenn myles ffrom Medfield about the latter end of June last did see a company of Indians come to ye ffarme afforsaid & did request to have Liquors ffor saving of some wolves but Nathaniell Mott w[d] not give y[m] any but tendered y[m] a pecke of Corne apeece to every y[m] ffor their paines in deliveringe the wolves but they refused & were so earnest ffor Liquors that one of the deponents was fforced to thrust them out of doores & told y[m] y[t] they would not be orderly he would laye handes y[m]."

The record of his marriage mentions him as a "Carpenter" of Roxbury. In 1674 he or his father resided a short time in Marblehead.

20 Feb., 1676–7. Wm. Bartholomew, carpenter, of Roxbury, and wife Mary, sell a twenty-five acre lot, house, etc., in Roxbury. He was at Deerfield before King Philip's war, purchasing the houselot previously belonging to Peter Woodward, which he sold in 1685.

At the time of the noted raid of the Indians on Hatfield, 19 Sept., 1677, he was there with his family, and probably assisting in the erection of the building then being raised. His daughter Abigail, aged four, was taken

8

with twelve others and carried through the forests, over the Lakes, into Canada and kept eight months; but finally, ransomed, 23 May, 1678, with others by the payment of £200.

"Att Eleven of the Clock in ye day time the enemy came upon Hatfield (When ye greatest part of the men belonging to the Towne were dispersed into ye meadows) and Shott down 3 men within ye Towne fortification, killed and took women & children & burnt houses & Barnes ye number of which are as followeth"

Killed (male) 12; taken 13, including "A child of Wm Barthemew^s^;" wounded 4. (From Sam'l Partridge's letter to the General Court.)

He is mentioned in Deerfield in 1678.

May 5, 1679. The town records of Branford, Conn., contain the following resolution: "The town have agreed to give unto William Bartholomew twenty acres of land as convenient as may be provided it be not prejudicial to ye Town provided also he do perfect his agreement with the Town Comt[ee] concerning building a mill in Branford and build and settle in the town. And Cap[n] Topping, Tho[s] Harrison, Robert Hoott & W[m] Hoadley or any 3 of them are appointed for a comt[ee] to treat and bargain with Mr. Bartholomew concerning building and upholding a mill in Branford and do give them full power to act in ye behalf of ye town."

Mr. Bartholomew must have gone there that summer as the committee, 5 Jan., 1679, was authorized to lay out to W[m] Bartholomew land below Guilford Road, and the following spring, 18 March, 1679–80, the town further granted him the "piece of upland & meadow lying between the brook that carried ye water from ye old mill and the stream that carried away ye waste water."

Feb. 7, 1681. "The Towne have given liberty to W[m]

Bartholomew to set up a saw mill upon the great river about the foot of the great hill and the town have given him liberty to make use of what timber he shall sea raise for sawing half a mile below said mill and so on both sides of the river and along his mill as far as he shall see cause."

March 11, 1683. Seventeen acres were laid out to him.

Aug. 11. "Wm Bartholomew was appointed to go to the bay to do his utmost indeavor to procure a minister for the town . . . . he being formerly appointed thereunto."

Nov. 1. He was "Chosen and appointed to keep ordinary in Branford." Only the best men then received such appointments.

1684. "The town have allowed William Bartholomew twelve acres of land . . in consideration of w^t^ time & money he hath expended for the procurement of a minister in year 1683." Also appointed Surveyor for the town.

June 17, 1684. "Whereas William Hoadley and William Bartholomew are now intending to go to the bay: The Towne do ord^r^ and commissionate the said men to do their utmost endeavor for the procurement of an orthodox minister to carry on the worke of the ministry in Branford and to take the best advice that may be for the attaining of the end aforesaid and do give them full power to act for and in the behalf of the towne."

1685. Wm Bartholomew and John Frisbie laid out and staked the highway to Guilford. Elected Surveyor again, —and Fence Viewer. Appointed to lay out and value certain tracts of land.

March 28, 1686–7. Another Mill agreement.

Jan. 2, 1687. Town object to his dam and want him to build a bridge. Ten acres more are laid out to him.

April 27, 1687. The town of Woodstock is anxious to obtain his services and passes the following resolution:

"The Company of Planters att a Gen[ll] Meeting did then choose Edw[d] Morris, John Chandler, Sen[r]., Nath[ll] Johnson & Joseph White, to treatt and agree with William Bartholomew of Branford for the building of a corn mill on as reasonable terms as they can, which terms the Publique is to stand to; and each man to bere his equal proportion according to his home lott."

"The Committee abovesaid did in the Town's behalf give and grant to W[m] Bartholomew above said, on condition of his building a corn mill on the falls below Muddy Brook ponds and finding the Town with grinding good meal clear of gritt as other towns have generally found these following particulars

1 the place at the aforesaid falls to sett a mill wth the benefit of the streams.

2 A fifteen acre home lott with 15 acre right of upland and a thirty acre right of meadow.

3 an hundred acres of upland . . . "

The Woodstock people were anxious to have the company of his good wife Mary and passed the following:

Sep. 29. "It was granted att a full meeting of the proprietors: that William Bartholomew should have twenty acres of land . . . . provided he bring his wife & settle upon it by next June following: . . "

Tracts were also granted to each of his sons Isaac and William.

Mar. 12, 1688. He was appointed on a "Com[ee] to settle highways."

May 21, 1688. Allowed more cow pasture in Branford.

July 13, 1689. "W[m] Bartholomew Sr." was commissioned by the governor of the colony of Massachusetts, ensign of the "New Roxbury Company."

Feb. 12, 1689–90. He, with three others, petitions the General Court for town privileges. The petition was granted and "Nepmuck" or "New Roxbury" was called Woodstock.

Oct. 1690. He was made chairman of a committee to build the minister a house; also, Nov. 1690, one of the first selectmen of the town.

May 21, 1691. "Wm Bartholomew being presented for Lieutenant and Benjamin Sabin for ensign of the *Military* Company in Woodstock the said persons are approved and confirmed in their respective offices." [Mass. Court Rec., Vol. 6, p. 184.]

June 8, 1692. "Mr. Wm Bartholomew" appeared as the representative of Woodstock, Suffolk County, at the Grand General Court or Assembly at Boston. It was the only one ever held by the colony and called on an extremely important occasion. It was also the occasion of the first election in Woodstock for representative, making it a conspicuous honor to Mr. Bartholomew, as the town was noted for its able citizens.

1690–1694. At the several divisions of the public land he was a member of the committee making the same and received with his sons Isaac and William their shares.

May 16, 1695. He was appointed with Benj. Sabin to join the Roxbury Committee "in staking and setting the divided line between the inhabitants of Roxbury & Woodstock."

Spring of 1697. Mr. Bartholomew died, probably in Woodstock; and it is supposed that his remains lie buried in Woodstock Hill Cemetery, adjoining the graves of his sons Joseph and Benjamin. Two rough unmarked stones at the head of graves probably show his and his son John's last resting places.

Lieutenant William Bartholomew was eminently a

practical man, and of good family and education ; his father a merchant, he preferred to learn the trade of a carpenter. After a life of several years in the metropolis of the colony he chose the rough and hazardous but useful lot of a frontier settler.

He was unfortunate in settling in Hatfield as the war with the savages during the several succeeding years made that locality uninhabitable.

He suffered severely by this war and finally seeking a more peaceable section in which to use his energies, made arrangements with the town of Branford, Ct., to build and maintain mills there.

Nearly forty years of his life had passed, the latter being unfortunately devoted to settlements in which it was impossible to succeed. In Branford his force of character had a better field ; and during the eight years spent there, besides building two mills and opening two farms, he was constantly called into service by the citizens and filled many important trusts.

But although nearly fifty years old and very comfortably situated, his ambition required him to accept the very generous offer of his old Roxbury acquaintances, who had settled in Woodstock, and there build and maintain mills for them.

His popularity was even greater in Woodstock than it had been in Branford. They conferred upon him nearly every honor at their disposal : making him selectman, chairman of the committee to build the minister's house, first representative to the General Court, and Lieutenant commanding all subject to military service in the town ; these honors, conferred by those who had known him from boyhood, are ample evidences of his superior character.

The social excellence of his family is certified to most

emphatically by the offer of a land grant if he would bring them there to live.

He died at the age of fifty-seven; and, judging by the age of his father and descendants his death must have been greatly hastened by some cause, possibly exposure during his trying times in the Indian wars.

Like his father he was ancestor of all the Bartholomews of this family in America. He as well as his father and uncle Henry must have been men of rare executive ability, which combined with their practical sense and high moral and social standard made them in their various spheres the eminent men which they undoubtedly were.

Few men have proved more worthy of being remembered and revered by their descendants.

Children of William and Mary (Johnson) Bartholomew were:

8 i Isaac[3], b. 1 Nov., 1664; d. 25 Oct., 1727.

ii William, b. 16 Oct., 1666; bapt. 21 Oct., 1666. He was in Woodstock with his father, receiving several grants of land there. Joined the church in Branford in 1692, and died before 1697, without issue, as inferred from his father's will. His Woodstock property was inherited by his brothers.

iii Mary, b. 26 Oct., 1668; bapt. 1 Nov., 1668; d. before 1697, leaving no children, as inferred from her father's will.

9 iv Andrew, b. 11 Dec., 1670; d. about 1755.

v Abigail, b. 8 Dec., 1672; m. 1st, 11 Jan., 1691-2, (fourth marriage entry on the record), in Woodstock, Joseph Frizzel of Woodstock (son of James F. of Roxbury) who dying, 13 May, 1704, she m. 2nd, in 1709,* Samuel[3] Paine (Stephen[2], Stephen[1]). She d. in W. 15 Jan., 1732, æt. 60. Sam'l Paine d. 11 May, 1735. She was stolen by the Indians. (See sketch of her father.)

---

*No date is mentioned in the records, but the following notice posted on the town post supplies the omission in a measure: "1708-9 Jan'y 18 Samuel Paine And Abigail Frissel both of Woodstock intend marriage."

1 John[4] Frizzel, b. 2 Sept., 1692.
2 Sarah Frizzel, b. 31 Jan., 1693-4.
3 Abigail Frizzel, b. 23 Oct., 1695.
4 Hannah Frizzel, b. 18 Oct , 1697.
5 Joseph Frizzel, b. 3 Oct., 1699.
6 Ebenezer Frizzel, d. 9 Nov., 1706.
7 Benjamin Frizzel, m. 9 March, 1732, H. Abbott; 2d, Naomi May.
8 Mary Frizzel.
9 Rebecca Paine, bapt. 15 July, 1710; m. 4 July, 1744, D. Cleveland.
10 Ebenezer Paine, bapt. 15 Oct., 1711; m. Mary Grosvinor 29 March, 1789.

vi Elizabeth , b. 15 Mar., 1674-5: bapt. 1 Mar., 1675: m. 21 Nov., 1699, in Woodstock, Edmund Chamberlain of W.

10 vii Benjamin , b. about 1677, probably in Hatfield.

11 viii John , b. about 1679.

12 ix Joseph , b. about 1682 in Branford.

In Roxbury, Lt. Bartholomew had received his first military rank. His initial rank was ensign. He had many mills including a mill in Woodstock, Connecticut. Many men from Roxbury, Massachusetts came down to Woodstock to work at the mill. It is seventy-two miles between the two towns, which takes a couple days to walk. The land in between was very rugged between Indians and wild animals.

It seems at first the Lt. Bartholomew lived in Roxbury or elsewhere initially but he moved to Woodstock at some point. He received his rank as lieutenant in Woodstock. He received this rank after the revolution of 1688 where King James II[69] was overthrown by an anti catholic, regime. The revolution was said to be bloodless, however the bloodlessness was specific to England. Ireland and Scotland both had massive losses of life. They were the start of the Whig Party in England, which was the commencement of Constitutional Monarchy and Parliamentary democracy.[70] After this time, would have been King William's War, which was a war against the French and Indian's. The battle was for land supremacy and fur trade routes. It is not for certain if Lt. Bartholomew actively fought in these battles but he did

---

69

https://connecticutgenealogy.com/windham/early_settlement_of_woodstock.htm

70

have some run ins per George Wells Bartholomew's book.[71]

As a Woodstock resident, Lt. Bartholomew did construction on homes and bridges. He also helped settle land disputes and was also elected as selectmen. There was a board of selectmen. They are the executive branches of towns in New England even now.[72]

William married Mary Johnson. Her grandfather was Captain John Johnson. He was a lowly man in England but he was the Captain of the first ship, which was part of the Great Immigration from England to the Americas. A passenger on his ship was Governor John Winthrop, the second governor of the Massachusetts Bay Colony. He was Surveyor General which some say was the highest military rank in the colonies at the time.[73]

Mary's father, Isaac, was a Captain of the Artillery. He'd been elected Captain of the Roxbury militia. He led the militia into battle of Fort Narragansett during King Phillip's War where he and eighty other militiamen were killed. The Indians lost over one thousand men.[74]

Mary has a pedigree of nobility. It's a rich history and a

---

[71] http://www.u-s-history.com/pages/h840.html The First of the French and Indian Wars

[72] Ibid Early Settlements

[73] https://familysearch.org/photos/artifacts/34957923

[74] www.americanancestors.org 2013: Early New England Families

strong history.

B.

Brand Geo. and Mathew Heath July 24. 1643.
Bowles John and Elizab. Heath Apr. 2. 1649
Bruce Danl. and Hannah Merrell Nov. 5. 1652
Bowen Henry and Elizab. Johnson Dec. 20. 1658
Brewer Nathl. and Elizab. Rand Dec. 1661
Bartholmew Willyam and Mary Johnson Dec. 17. 1663
Baker Thomas and Marie Gambling May 27. 1665
Brathers Ralph and Hannah Gore June 13. 1677
Bowles John and Sarah Eliot Nov. 16. 1681
Bishop Thomas and Anne Gary June 7. 1683
Bowen Henry and Susanna Heath Apr. 14. 1684
Buckminster Joseph and Martha Sharp May 12. 168
Bacon Joseph and Margaret Bowen Nov. 6. 1688
Bridge Edward and Mary Brooks May 27. 1690
Brewer Nathl. and Margaret Weld March 17. 169-
Beacon John and Abiel Curtiss Nov. 21. 1693.
Bacon Geo. and Mary Davis May 4. 1699
Benton Nicholas and Mary Ashdell 1700
Bacon Jacob and Dorothy Bradhurst Dec. 24. 1700
Bugbee Thomas and Sarah Peake June 4. 1701
Briggs Peter and Elizab. Atherton 1701
Baker Thomas and Sarah Pike May 28. 1702
Bird Abiel of Dorchester and Mindwell Weeks Jan. 24. 1
Brackett John and Rebecca Ruggles Apr. 10. 1705
Bacon Saml. of Dedham and Elizab. Ackers July 3. 170
Brewer Nathl. and Elizab. Sunderland Dec. 20. 1705

75

BARON, Moses (-1719, 1720) & Mary (**BUNKER**) **RICHARDSON** (-1741), w Ezekiel, m/3 Thomas **HOWE** of Marlboro; 2 Feb 1697/8; Chelmsford
BARRON, Timothy (1673-1718) & Rachel **JENISON** (1671-), m/2 John **KING** 28 Sep 1720; 10 Mar 1699; Watertown
BARROWS, George & Patience **SIMMONS** (-1723, Plympton); 14 Feb 1694/5; Plymouth
BARROWS/BARRY?, James & _?_, m/2 Niven **AGNEW** b 1676; b 1662?
BARROWS, John (1609-1692) & Ann _?_; b 1637; Salem/Middleboro
BARROWS, John (-1692) & Deborah _?_; b 1666; Plymouth
BAROW, John & Hannah **BRIGGS** (-1710?); 13 - 1698; Rochester
BARROWS, John & Sarah _?_; b 1700(1?); Plymouth
BARROW, Robert & 1/wf Ruth **BONUM/BONHAM**; 28 Nov 1666; Plymouth
BARROW, Robert & 2/wf Lydia [**DUNHAM**] (1666?-1717); b 1686; Plymouth
BARROWS, Samuel (1672-) & 1/wf Mercy **COMBS** (-1718); b 1701; Middleboro
BARRUS/BARROWS?, Joshaue & Mary **CHAMBERLING**; 24 Jul 1696; Chelmsford
BARSHAM, John (?1635, ?1641-1698) & Mahitable _?_; b 1670; Exeter, NH/Portsmouth, NH
BARSHAM, Nathaniel (-1716) & Elizabeth **BOND** (-1729); 13 Mar 1678, 1678/9, no issue; Watertown
BARSHAM, Philip (-1675) & Sarah _?_; Deerfield
BARSHAM, William (-1684) & Annabelle [**BLAND**]?, alias **SMITH** (-1681); ca 1634; Watertown
BASTOW, George (1614-1654) & Susanna [**MARRETT**] (-1654); b 1650; Boston/Scituate/Cambridge
BEARSTOW, George (1652-1726) & Mercy [**CLARK**] (1660-1726), dau James; b 1684; Roxbury/Boston/Rehoboth
BARSTOW, Jeremiah (-1676) & Lydia [**HATCH**] (1633?-), dau Thomas, m/2 Richard **STANDLAKE** ca 1677; b 1676; Scituate
BARSTOW, John (-1658, ae 33) & Hannah _?_; b 1653; Watertown/Cambridge
BARSTOW, John & Lydia **HATCH**, dau William; 16 Jan 1678; Scituate
BERSTOW, Joseph (?1639-1712) & Susanna **LINKHORNE/LINCOLN** (-1730), Hingham; 16 May 1666; Scituate
BEARSTOW, Joseph (1675-1728) & Mary [**RANDELL**]; b 1699; Scituate
BARSTOW, Michael/Miles? (1600-1676, 1674?) & Grace **HALSTEAD**; 16 Feb 1625, b 1635, 16 Feb 1624, 15 Feb 1624, no issue; Charlestown
BAIRSTOW, Michael/Mihel/etc. & Rachel **THAINE/TRAIN/TRAYNE**; 12 Jan 1676, 1676/7, 12 Dec 1676; Watertown
BAIRSTOW, William (1612-1668) & Ann **HUBBARD**, m/2 John **PRINCE** ca 1670; 8 Jul 1638; Dedham/Scituate
BERSTOW, William (1652-) & Sarah/?Martha _?_; b 1676(7?); Scituate
BARTER, Henry (-1747) & 1/wf Sarah [**CROCKET**]; Kittery, ME
BARTER, Peter & ?Margaret _?_; Star Island
BARTHOLOMEW, Andrew (1670-1755?) & Hannah [**FRISBIE**] (1682-); ca 1698?, b 1699; Branford, CT/Wallingford, CT
BARTHOLOMEW, Henry (-1622) (see Samuel **LOTHROP**) & Elizabeth [**SCUDDER**]? (-1682), dau Thomas; b 1641; Salem/Boston
BARTHOLOMEW, Henry (1657-1698) & Katherine [**HUTCHINSON**] (1653-), m/2 Richard **JANVERON**/?**CHAMBERLAIN** 1699; no issue; Salem
BARTHOLOMEW, Isaac (1664-1727) & Rebecca [?**FRISBIE**] (?1679, ?1676-1738, ae 62); ca 1694; Woodstock, CT/Branford, CT
BARTHOLOMEW, William (-1681, ae 78) & Anne/Mary? [**LORD**?] (-1683); b 1640, Woodstock, CT; Boston/Charlestown
BARTHOLOMEW, William (1640-) & Mary **JOHNSON** (1642-); 17 Dec 1663; Roxbury/Branford, CT
BARTLETT, Abijah & Captivity [**JENNINGS**] (1678-); b 1701?; Hadley
BARTLETT, Abraham (1666-) & Elizabeth [**JONES**], w James; by 1686; Portsmouth, NH
BARTLETT, Abraham (-1731) & Mary **WARNER** (1664-1738) Middletown; 11 Jun 1693; Guilford, CT
BARTLETT, Alexander & Sarah _?_; b 1676; Northampton
BARTLETT, Benjamin (1632-1691) & 1/wf Susanna [**JENNEY**]; ca 1655; Duxbury
BARTLETT, Benjamin (1632-1691) & 2/wf Sarah [**BREWSTER**]; ca 1656; Duxbury

[75] Massachuesetts, Town and Vital Statistics

Chapter 6 Joseph Bartholomew 1682-1724

12 Joseph[3] (*William,*[2] *William,*[1] *William*), born in Branford about 1682; married 12 Nov., 1713, Elizabeth, daughter of Nathaniel Sanger of Woodstock.

He was a farmer of Woodstock.

They both died on the same day and have a double gravestone inscribed as follows:

Here lies Buried y[e]	Here lies Buried y[e]
Body of Joseph Bartho-	Body of Elizabeth
lomew aged 42 years.	his wife aged 35 years.

They both died Oct. y[e] 15, 1724.

This stone adjoins the one supposed to designate Lieut. Wm. Bartholomew's grave.

Guardians were appointed that year for his children, Samuel, Joseph, Jedidiah, Mary, John and Benjamin.

They are also mentioned as scholars at Thaddeus Mason's school in Woodstock, between 1729 and 1739.

On May 23, 1742, Samuel was made guardian of his brothers and sisters. Children:

26 i Samuel[4], b. 2 Nov., 1714; lived in Saybrook, Ct.
27 ii Joseph, b. 10 Feb., 1715-6; res. in W. Woodstock.
iii Jedidiah, b. 30 Oct., 1717; 7 Oct., 1746, letters of administration were granted in Philadelphia, Pa., "to Joseph Spavin on the estate of the late Jedidiah Barthelmay dec'd." Among items in the inventory of estate of "Jedidiah Bartholomew" were "Dieting & Lodging dec'd 12 weeks at 8 s. per week 4£." "Liquors &c expended at his funeral 4£.
iv Mary, b. 10 Feb., 1718-9.
v John, b. 15 Mar., 1720-1, may have been the one referred to partly in items (see p. 76).
28 vi Benjamin, b. 23 June, 1723; d. 1801.

There is not a lot about Joseph Bartholomew other than what George Wells has printed. One comment on Joseph's Find A Grave entry states that researchers found the death of Joseph and Elizabeth was likely due to a fire, which spread throughout the house. It is curious though how the children all survived since they were all under the age of eighteen.[76]

[76] findagrave.com entry 47811988

Samuel Bugbee & Dorothy Carpenter, Jan. 26, 1701–2
David Bishop & Rebecca Hubbard, Feb. 4, 1701–2
Joseph Shaw of Stonington & Susannah Grosvenor of Mashamoquet, March 26, 1702
Christopher Peake & Mary Stratton, June 21, 1702
John Bartholomew & Elisabeth Morss, June 28, 1702
John Goodall & Lydia Titus, Nov. 10, 1702
Nathaniel Seshions of Pomfret & Hannah Corbin of Woodstock, March 2, 1706–7
Samuel Hemingway & Hannah Morris, Nov. 12, 1707
Jonathan Payson & Mary Cook, Jan. 12, 1709–10
Samuel Gates & Mary Truesdale, both of Pomfret, Feb. 12, 1709–10
John Goodell & Hannah Colburn, Oct. 8, 1710
Benjamin Goodell & Hannah Gary, both of Pomfret, May 22, 1711
Robert Mayson & Hannah Holmes, Nov. 15, 1711
John Chamberlain & Esther Alcock, Nov. 24, 1711
John May of W. & Elizabeth Child of Brookline, Mass., Dec. 18, 1711
Leicester Grosvenor & Mary Hubbard, both of Mashemoquet, Jan. 16, 1711-12
Jessie Carpenter & Mary Bacon, Feb. 27, 1711
Jeremiah Sabin & Abigail Davis, both of Pomfret, May 8, 1712
Robert Buck of Killingly & Elizabeth Bacon of W., June 8, 1712
John Marcy & Experience Colburn, Jan. 14, 1712-13
John March of Mendon & Abigail Eastman of W., Jan. 15, 1712-13
Samuel Carpenter of Pomfret & Hannah Johnson of W., Feb. 4, 1713
Ebenezer Eastman ot W. & Sarar Pease of Haverhill, June 3, 1713
Joseph Bartholomew & Elizabeth Sanger, Nov. 12, 1713

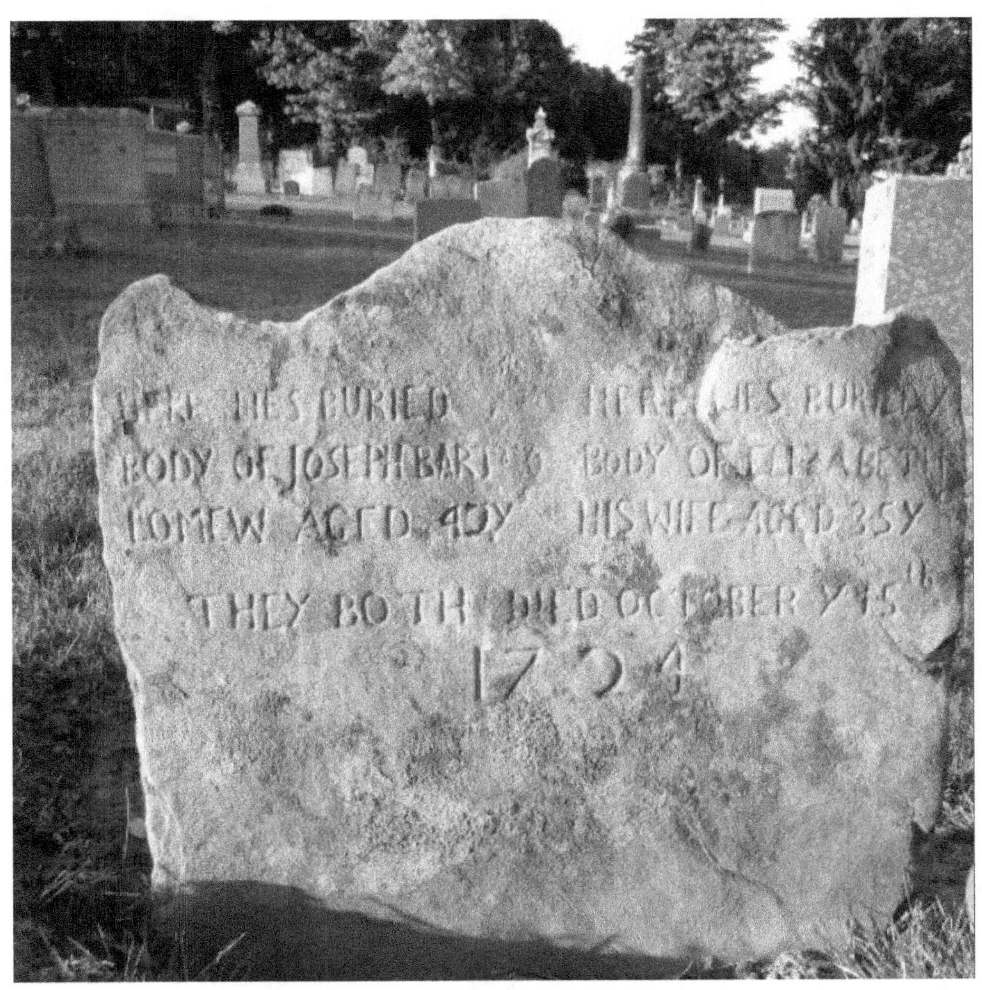
BODY OF JOSEPH BART
THEY BOTH DIED OCTOBER

Chapter 7 Samuel Bartholomew 1714-Unknown

26 Samuel[4] (*Joseph,*[3] *William,*[2] *William,*[1]) born in

Samuell Bartholomew (1737.)

Woodstock, 2 Nov., 1714; married Hannah———.

He was made guardian of his brothers and sister 23 May, 1742. He bought and sold several tracts of Woodstock land between 1737 and 1741; the last being for £1244. The following record is based mainly upon the memory of Mr. Levi Bartholomew.

Samuel Bartholomew was a sea captain, making Saybrook, Ct., his home. He died "while his children were young," and his remains are said to have been "buried on some shore."

Mrs. Hannah married, second, a Mr. Jones and was still living within the memory of her grandson Levi, in Oswego county, N. Y. Children:

i Elijah[5] bought land and settled in Middlefield, Mass., in Nov., 1787; dying unm. before 1 May, 1792, when Aaron Gillett of Hebron, Ct., was made administrator of his estate.

ii Gideon, m. and had two children born before 1797, who remained in Conn. after he removed to Oswego Co., N. Y. Was an expert violinist.

iii Hannah,

65 iv William, b. 1759–60; d. 21 Sept., 1822.

66 v Samuel, b. 1762–3; d. 12 Dec., 1740, æt. 77.

Chapter 8 Samuel Bartholomew 1762-1840

66 Samuel[5] (*Samuel*[4], *Joseph*[3], *William*[2],) born in Saybrook, Ct., about 1762; married, 13 Jan., 1784, Elizabeth Butler of Waterford, Ct.; and died 12 Dec., 1840, æt. 78. She was born in 1757 and died 27 May, 1846, æt. 83.

Mr. Bartholomew was left fatherless when a child; was apprenticed when a boy, abused and ran away. He enlisted when seventeen; the company being rendezvoused at Waterford, Ct. He served in the regiments of Colonels Sherman and Huntington, at Fort Putnam and at West Point and that vicinity, for three years.

After the war, and his marriage, he settled near his wife's home in Waterford, then a parish in the town of New London. About 1800, he moved to Unadilla, Otsego Co., N. Y., where both he and his wife died. Both were members of the Methodist Church, she having been baptized in W. 8 May, 1794. Children:

178 i John,[6] b. 3 Apr., 1788; d. 16 Jan., 1865, æt. 76.
179 ii Levi, b. 25 July, 1797; lives in Unadilla, æt. 86.
180 iii Samuel, b. 23 Mar., 1803; d. 17 Dec., 1878, æt. 75.
iv Rebecca, m. Samuel Smith; and d. in Unadilla. Of ch., Leander[7] and Edward moved west; Jarvis, Gilbert and Hannah (Taylor) live in Unadilla.
v Hannah, m. John Smith; and d. at Butternuts, N. Y.
1 Levi Smith, resides in Binghampton, N. Y.

2 George Smith, resides in Unadilla.
3 Rebecca Smith, m. 1st, John Haynes; 2nd, — Raynor; res. U. Ch. (1) Wellington of Butternuts, (2) Hannah (d.), Haynes.
4 Lucy Smith, m. 1st, — Bowing; 2nd, Parker Smith; res. U. Ch. (1) Alonzo.
vi David, always an invalid; d. unm. ab. 1850.

Samuel Bartholomew joined the military per George Wells Bartholomew at the age of seventeen. It is important to understand how the Colonial Connecticut Militia worked.

The Militia was raised in Connecticut in 1739. People who signed up in the military joined a company and the company they joined was based in the town they joined in. John was part of the Waterford Company. These companies were part of a regiment. They would train in their own towns with their officer, and then they would gather with others in their regiment and train as a regiment under their regiment commander.

In times of war, like the Revolutionary War, the regiments would join forces called a brigade under a brigadier general.

The Brigadier general would command the brigade. A major, lieutenant colonel and colonel would command the regiments. The company commanders would be lieutenant, like William Bartholomew, earlier, ensign, sergeant and corporal.[77]

---

[77] http://connecticutsar.org/understanding-the-connecticut-militia/

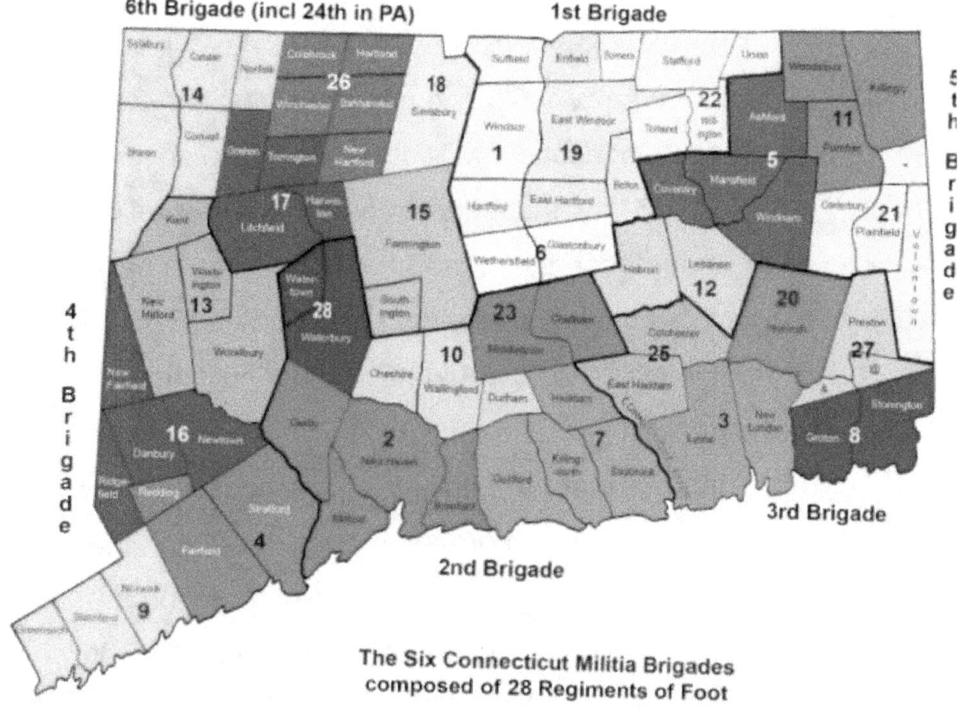

The Six Connecticut Militia Brigades composed of 28 Regiments of Foot

The commander of the third regiment during Samuel's service was Colonel Jonathan Latimer. He was the Commander from 1776 to 1783.[78] Prior to Samuel's enlistment, Col. Latimer charged his regiment into Bunker Hill. He also did tours in the French and Indian War.[79] How long Samuel was in the third regiment. Since enlistments were three years, some people did not re-up. This caused realignments. Some of this caused the Brigade numbers to change as well as regiment numbers.

---

78 https://allthingsliberty.com/2016/07/connecticut-militia-1739-1783/

79 ibid familysearch.org L6VK-MXQ

The Brigadier General was John Tyler. He joined the Continental Army 1776 and became Brigadier General. As part of the Connecticut Militia, he promoted several times, prior to 1776.[80] It is not known how long Samuel would have been under these two. If he had been it would have been at the very beginning of service. Based on the Record of Bartholomew's these would have been his immediate commanders.

There were some realignments, which occurred.[81] This is why it seems this information does not match that of George Wells Bartholomew. Under the realignment, the Connecticut 3rd Regiment was brought into the 20th Continental Foot (infantry) Regiment. General Huntington, mentioned in George Wells's book is, was in command of the 20th Continental Regiment.

Their job in the 20th Continental was to secure the West Point along the Hudson River. The West Point was aptly named that because it was the western pointed section along the Hudson, across from Constitutional Island,

---

80

http://freepages.genealogy.rootsweb.ancestry.com/~pyle/GBR/JOHN_S_TYLER .html

81 Wright, Richard K. (1983). "Lineage". *The Continental Army*. Army Lineage Series. United States Army Center of Military History. CMH Pub 60-4. Retrieved 5 June 2006

Connecticut.

Constitutional Island was a Garrison post for protection of the waterways to northern New York and New England. It was one of the early lines of defense for where General George Washington was headquartered, prior to any fortification of the West Point.

After Sir Henry Clinton handily moved up the Hudson in 1777. He took control of Constitutional Island, it was understood how important the control of the Hudson would be. Not only for passage, but it would split the colonies in half if the Regular British Army controlled the Hudson. After short occupation, General Clinton retreated back to British headquarter in New York City. The retreat was brought about because of the capture of another British General at Saratoga.

General Washington saw an opportunity to regain the southern posts on the Hudson. He fortified the Hudson Highlands on the west from the Tappan Zee down to Newburgh. He declared the West Point to be the most important Post in the war.

Up to that time, the West Point had not been fortified. Even though winter had fallen, and it was a brutally cold winter at that, troops worked tirelessly. Supplies had been brought in from twenty miles away for fortification.

The way the river bends west to east at that point, it was the narrowest part of the river. The West Point had a strategic advantage over the river. As a Highland, it made the West Point harder to infiltrate than Constitutional Island. Because it came to a point in the Hudson, it gave a clear view, north and south. No British vessels could come up the Hudson without the West Point Post knowing about it. Even if the British were able to get into the bend, they would never make it through. They would have received heavy fire from the West Point and from the newly refortified Constitutional Island.

Fort Putnam, Fort Clinton and many other fortifications were double downed on, along the Hudson. This is why foot regiments like Samuel's were so important at the time.

As soon as the West Point Post fortification was complete, and troops were in place, General Washington moved his headquarters to the West Point. This was strategic because of all the military posts and Garrisons; the West Point was centrally located along the Hudson River. It became the most secure location along the Hudson.

In 1780, Major General Benedict Arnold was given command of the operations of the West Point. It was shortly after General Arnold had taken command of West Point that he preceded in negotiations to sell West Point and the land it was on, to the British.[82]

Based on when Colonel Huntington would have been at West Point, it is most likely that Samuel Bartholomew would have been at West Point when General Washington had moved his headquarters there and certainly when Benedict Arnold would have tried to sell West Point. Fort Putnam was considered a West Point Fortification and used to stop any advances North towards West Point and Albany. Huntington was also part of the board at the trial for Arnold. Huntington however would have been Samuel's colonel for a brief time. Based on his estimated birth year and that he enlisted at seventeen, there's not a lot of time he could have been under Huntington. There are several military roll calls that were taken and still preserved that have Samuel under Sherman for an extended period of time almost back to when Samuel was seventeen.

Colonel Jedidiah Huntington would have been his first commander. He had been the commander of the 20th

---

[82] Palka, Colonel Eugene & Galgano, Colonel Francis Jr.; *The Military Geography of Fortress West Point* United States Military Academy, West Point 2001 pp all

Everything about West Point Including Benedict Arnold was from this publication which is also found with helpful maps at

http://www.westpoint.edu/gene/siteassets/sitepages/publications/the%20military%20geography%20of%20fortress%20west%20point%202001.pdf

Connecticut Foot Regiment prior to Samuel's enlistment.[83] In 1779, Huntington's Brigade was ordered to the highlands in Connecticut opposite the Hudson from West Point. His Brigade's sole purpose was to continue building redoubts in support of West Point. Some of these redoubts were set up to protect against advances from the British advancing. The British had made some raids on Connecticut coastal cities to draw Washington and the Continental Army out of the highlands. Some troops from the Connecticut line had gone to support but the British had withdrawn by the time the Connecticut line came.[84]

In 1781, General Washington commanded the Connecticut, New Hampshire and Massachusetts lines to hold the Highlands in the Hudson. During this time, Washington led the siege against Yorktown, which effectively ended the war.[85]

Huntington, by this point had become Brigadier General. In June of 1783 near the ending of the war, Huntington was one of the few remaining generals left at the West Point. It was near the same time he received brevet as Major

---

[83] https://allthingsliberty.com/2016/07/connecticut-militia-1739-1783/

[84] Johnston, A.M. (1889). *Record of Connecticut Men in the Military and Naval Service during the War of the Revolution*. Hartford, CT. p. 19.

[85] Johnston, A.M. (1889). *Record of Connecticut Men in the Military and Naval Service during the War of the Revolution*. Hartford, CT. p. 19.

General.[86]

Benedict Arnold is important to US history as well a Bartholomew history. He's important because Samuel Bartholomew's grandson's, Chauncey Bartholomew, married Sarah Jacox. The Jacox line can be traced, through the Hazzard line, to Governor Benedict Arnold, great, great uncle to the General Benedict Arnold. Governor Benedict Arnold was governor of Colonial Rhode Island.

The other place George Wells Bartholomew mentions that Samuel Bartholomew was stationed was Fort Putnam. In many sources, Fort Putnam is considered part of West Point. Fort Putnam was considered a redoubt for the West Point and would have been off location. It would have been used as an outpost for the initial post. It was a place of retreat and protection for the main line but also as a line of protection before the main post, in this case, West Point. Because it would be free standing, it would have had it's own commander.[87] Huntington likely would have commanded at Fort Putnam and Fort Putnam was likely one of the redoubts that Huntington and Samuel would have been a part of.

A description of Fort Putnam's function is as follows:

Fort Putnam was a Revolutionary War fort built on Crown Hill at West Point to protect Fort Clinton and the plain below from a land attack. Construction began on 11 Apr 1778 as one of two principal forts,

---

[86] Huntington, Elijah B. (1863). *A genealogical memoir of the Huntington family*. p. 161.

[87] https://en.wikipedia.org/wiki/Redoubt

> designed to withstand a 10 day siege. Ramparts originally constructed with dry stone masonry later reinforced with lime mortar. Interior included three casemates, two bomb proofs and a provision magazine. Garrison planned at 420 men most to be housed in tents and huts outside the fort. Armed in 1780 with five 18 pounders, two 12 pounder, two 6 pounders, one 4 pounder and four 5.5" mortars[88].

Colonel Isaac Sherman was a commander at West Point, proper. In August of 1779, Sherman requested from Washington to return to the line from West Point.[89] In 1780, he took command of the newly realigned 5th Regiment of Connecticut. It consisted of eight battalion companies and one light infantry company. That company followed Washington into New York City[90]. Nothing indicates that Samuel Bartholomew saw any action in New York City.

However, Sherman must have returned to the West Point because on the roll calls, he was shown as Samuel's General. Whatever battles he would have fought in New

---

[88] http://www.fortwiki.com/Fort_Putnam_(1)

[89] Fitzpatrick, John C., *Calendar of the Correspondence of George Washington, Commander in Chief of the Continental Army, with the Officers October 19, 1778- December 20, 1780 Vol. 2.* Government Printing Office, Washington DC p1119

[90] http://www.5cr.org/index_files/5cr_history.htm 5cr stands for 5th Connecticut Regiment

York City might have earned him a promotion. The roll calls also show Samuel at West Point for the duration of the time he was under Sherman. The rolls that are known are from 1781-1783. During that period of time both Samuel and General Sherman's whereabouts are confirmed one hundred percent.

His chain of command under General Sherman started with Captain Nehemiah Rice. Most of the rolls show him under Rice. Other sources show him under Rice including books by the daughters of the revolution. Another Samuel Bartholomew served but in a different state under a different set of commanders so this proves the information concerning Private Samuel Bartholomew to be accurate.[91] There is not a lot out there as to Captain Rice's involvement in the war specifically to trace where Samuel would have been other than the second formation of the 5th Regiment at West Point.

Towards the end of the war, Samuel's captain switched from Captain Rice to Captain Stilwell. Samuel's gravestone, given to him by Daughters of the Revolution, states he was part of Stillwell's Militia in New Jersey. However, Captain Stillwell from New Jersey was Jeremiah Stillwell. Per the rolls, the captain of the Connecticut Regiment was Elias

[91] National Society of the Daughter's of the Revolution *National Lineage Book* Washington, 1921 p 154 entry 5754 May Smith Matthews

Stilwell. This is confirmed on the muster rolls in September of 1783 still under the Connecticut 2nd Regiment and under General Sherman still. Some records state Huntington was also involved in the 2nd Regiment. With there only being a few regiments left, it could be some overlap especially since Huntington and Sherman were both in the Highlands of the Hudson River. Connecticut stayed back to protect the Highlands with Washington's final advances to end the war.[92]

After the War, Samuel Bartholomew married Elizabeth Butler in Connecticut in 1784. They moved to New York because Samuel received a tract of land from the US Treasury Department as part of his pension for serving in the Revolutionary War. The land was in Unadilla, Otsego, New York.

Below is a photo of the letter, Samuel's son, Levi wrote on his behalf concerning his pension. Much of the writing is illegible but what is legible is very important. Some thought the letter was written in 1892 however if It's studied closer there is a # sign before the 1892 which seems to be a street number before the street. 1892 is an actual street number on New Road in Delaware County, New York.

---

[92] Jacobus, Donald; Curry, Kate *Revolutionary War Records of Fairfield Connecticut* Baltimore, 2004 p. 331, 332

Samuel has two headstones on his grave. There is one that is worn away and thought to be the original. There is a new one that was donated by the Daughter's of the Revolution. The birthday's and death days are the same. The information DAR provided is correct except the Militia. It says on his gravestone he was in Stillwell's militia in New Jersey. The error is not made on the researcher, as there is more than enough evidence to prove he was in Stillwell's Militia in Connecticut. There were other people with the Bartholomew surname and Samuel for a first name who was in the revolutionary war. And as we saw with George Well's Bartholomew, the wrong person could be assigned in a generation. Joseph and William, who were brothers, both had sons named Samuel, and grandsons named Samuel and great grandson's named John. George mixed this up on John, great grandson of Joseph. If there is not careful research with cross checking, it is easy to get information mixed up. From all the research and cross-referencing, even though the gravestone says New Jersey, that information is not correct. But it is in fact the same Samuel Bartholomew in the family lineage.

There is not a ton of information about Samuel's wife, Elizabeth Butler. What we do know about her was written in letters trying to obtain Samuel's pension. Many letters were written by the county judge on her behalf to the US pension office. What is gathered is that the pension office did not think Elizabeth married Samuel. There was no marriage license or certificate.

From secondary sources such as George Wells Bartholomew who interviewed children and grandchildren of Samuel and Elizabeth not much information was gleaned about Elizabeth.

What these letters brought, however, were dates of the wedding, details about the wedding, who was at the wedding, the location of the wedding right down to who preformed the ceremony. Two of Elizabeth's sisters wrote sworn affidavits describing details about the wedding. Both sisters give their first names. One letter also included Elizabeth's father's name, Joseph. The wedding was a Baptist wedding done at Joseph's house. The minister who said he didn't keep any record of marriage at the time remembered marrying the two in Connecticut wrote another affidavit. One letter included her own words, which were written by the judge. She was not literate so she made her sign between her first and last name. Her sign was similar to Samuel's as he was also illiterate. Both made an x connected by an arch on top much like a ribbon.

The same judge who wrote letters on behalf of Elizabeth had written a letter on behalf of Samuel. The letter read that Samuel was sick and incapable of working any longer. The plea was that since Samuel had given so much to his country in service of the revolutionary war, could the country please help him with a pension. Pensions for revolutionary war heroes were not granted until after the War of 1812. Shortly after the petition for aid from his country, Levi Bartholomew writes the above letter with a request for monetary pension.

Capt. Nehemiah Rice's Co.,

5 Reg't Conn Troops

(2d Formation, 1781.)

(Revolutionary War.)

Company Muster Roll.

CAPTION OF ROLL.

Muster Roll of Captain Nehemiah Rice's Company 5 Connecticut Regiment in the service of the United States of North America Commanded by Lt Colonel Commandant Sherman for January 1781

CERTIFICATE.

Feb 6 1781 Then mustered Capt Nehemiah Rice's Company as specified in the above roll

Jno. Heath M B & Sub Insp
Conn Brigade

ENDORSEMENT.

Muster Roll of Captain Rice's Company 5 Connecticut Regiment for January 1781

Camp.

(5435) [OVER.] Copyist.

Tho the
Treasury Department
Third auditors office

February 27th 1849
Newroad Delaware
County New York

Dear Sir

my farther
Samuel Bartholamew was a Revolutionary Soildier and drew $96 pens when he was dischard he had dead of a lot of land he thought it was so far off that it wont good for enny thing to see farm it got destroyed were I was quite young boy I number of his [illegible] of the [illegible] having it to play with

If it aint contrary to the Rules of your office I wish you would in form me when the Land was given to him and what ~~number the lot was and the statement~~ of all that is nessary so that I can find out where the Land is and whether it is setteld by eny one and you will obliege your most obedient sir
your Respect fully

Levi Bartholamew
Newroad Delaware
County New York

The original gravestone

above

Chapter 9 John Bartholomew 1788-1865

178 John[6] (*Samuel*[5], *Samuel*[4], *William*[3],) born in that part of Saybrook, now Waterford, Ct., 3 April, 1788; married Lydia, daughter of Asa Maynard, a descendant of the Pilgrim Captain, Miles Standish, and died 16 Jan., 1865, æt. 76.

She was born 26 Feb., 1798; died 28 Feb., 1874, æt. 76. Mr. Bartholomew was a farmer in Unadilla, N. Y. Children:

366 i Chauncey[7], b. 23 Apr., 1816; res. Sidney Plains, N. Y.
ii Achel, b. 22 Feb., 1817; d. 28 Jan., 1836.
iii Buania, b. 23 May, 1820; m. Charles Butler; res. Unadilla. Ch.
1 Handmaid A.[8] Butler.
iv Frederick Dan, b. 8 Aug., 1822; was crippled when a boy by a rolling log; d. unm. 28 Nov., 1863, in Unadilla.
367 v Zara Dan, b. 3 June, 1824; res. Animus City, Colo.
vi John, b. 3 July, 1826; m. Elsie Hall of Sherburn, N. Y.; res. Columbus Centre, Chenango Co., N. Y.; one son and two daughters.
vii Eliza Ann, b. 6 July, 1829; d. unm. 17 Sept., 1853.
viii Lydia Ann, b. 16 May, 1832; m. 22 Aug., 1852, Lewis E. Cobb; res. Blaine, Portage Co., Wis. Ch.
1 Harriett E. Cobb, b. 7 Dec., 1854; m. 14 Feb., 1874, B. W. Edwards.
2 Charles E. Cobb, b. 23 Dec., 1855.
3 Lucia Cobb, b. 6 Sept., 1857.
4 Velonia J. Cobb, b. 14 Nov., 1860.
5 Starr F. Cobb, b. 23 Jan., 1864.
6 Rena Cobb, b. 23 Dec., 1868.
7 Ruth V. Cobb, b. 5 Sept., 1877.
ix Andrew Jackson, b. 16 Sept., 1834; was in Co. D, 89th N. Y. V. Regt., and wounded at the battle of Antietam, dying six weeks after, 5 Nov., 1862, at Frederick City, Md.; never married.
368 x Truman Achel, b. 6 Sept., 1836; res. St. Edwards, Neb.
369 xi Ambrose Games, b. 31 March, 1840; res. Shelton, Neb.

As seen above, this shows generation three as William when generation three is Joseph. There are two things to look at with this, from George Wells's book alone. Under Samuel, grandson of Joseph, son of Samuel, it lists Samuel's sons and one is John. George also divides his book by generation. In the generations the siblings are grouped together. Cousins are grouped together and fanned out from there. The others on either side of John who are siblings to John, and listed as siblings of John in Samuel's section, have generation three listed as Joseph. DAR and SAR both have lineages that run through John to Samuel.

One interesting thing, which George Wells points out, is Lydia Maynard, John's wife, is a descendant of Captain Miles Standish. Researching her lineage on first glance, the claim couldn't be substantiated. Reversing the lineage and beginning with Miles Standish proved fruitless because each generation had multiple children.

A simple search netted a DNA test, which did tie Lydia to Captain Miles Standish. The layout of the DNA descendants is very hard to go through but it does show the link. The names tree do not match what else is out there, however the DNA tree would net pretty accurate results if there were enough entries from accurate family trees, aside from the one obtained for the majority of this research.

Ancestry expert, Nina Sheets stated, sometimes public records get messed up because sometimes children lived with aunts and uncles or other family members. When census takers would come, they would list all the children in a household as children of the head of house. Other people might have more accurate public records with other sources, cross-referenced with DNA can have a solid family tree to connect other people. The Standish family tree is very well documented. If they have done DNA testing for other branches on the tree, it can tie things together better.[93]

Lydia's father was Asa Maynard. His father was Jotham Maynard II: his father was Jotham Maynard: His father was David Maynard: his father was John Maynard II. John Maynard II, born in 1637 and died in 1711, married Mary Gates. Mary Gates, born 1636 and died in 1682 was daughter to Stephen Gates (1599-1662) and Anne Neave (1603-1683). They are on the DNA results, which are related to Miles Standish.

Anne Neave had variations of her maiden name. There were inconclusive results that depending on a variant she might descend from Bartholomew de Badlesmere. The theory is that her maiden name is a miss spelling of Veare, a descendant of De vere who are direct descendants of de Badlesmere. Two generations prior to hers can be directly linked back to the earliest Badlesmere.

---

[93] Sheets, Nina *Interview* Anderson 2017

The one thing about nobility and royalty is that it was a small group of people even when including multiple nations. The fact that Lydia had suspect of some nobility and royalty in one line it was easier to substantiate in other lines.

One line in particular tied her definitely to Badlesmere but also to the Plantagenet dynasty, which ties into more royalty and nobility naturally.

Jotham Maynard Sr 1714-1773 (Abiel Allen 1718-1773) Abiel was the daughter of Ephraim Allen 1691-1776 and Susanna Beacon 1695-1762. From this point, The Beacon/Bacon family connects to many. Susanna was the daughter of John Bacon 1670-1713 and Abiel Curtis 1676-1744.

Following the Curtis line we follow Abiel's father, Philip Curtis 1632-1675, son of William, 1592-1672, son of Thomas, 1560-1605. Thomas married Mary Camp 1560-1594 daughter of Richard Camp 1540-1569 and Magdalene Hall (no dates) daughter of Richard Hall 1511-1602, son of Robert Hall 1458- and Anna de Dudley 1460-1523. Anna was daughter of John Sutton Lord Dudley 1427-1503, son of John 1400-1487, son of John 1381-1406, son of John 1361-1395, son of John 1338-1370 and Katherine Stafford 1347-1361. She was the daughter of Sir Ralph Stafford 1301-1372 and

Margaret Audley 1301-1349. Margaret was daughter to Hugh Audley 1289-1347 and Margaret de Clare 1293-1342. Margaret was daughter to Gilbert de Clare 1240-1298 and Joan de Acre 12-72-1307. Joan de Acre received de Acre from her place of birth when her parents visited the Holy Land during the Crusades. Her father was King Edward Longshanks of the Plantagenet Dynasty.

Five generations back from Joan, Geoffrey Plantagenet 1113-1151 married Adelaide Matilda Beauclerc 1102-1167, daughter of King Henry Beauclerc and granddaughter to William Beauclerc known also as William the Conqueror. Henry married into Scottish royalty with the marriage of King Malcom III's (Dunkeld Dynasty) daughter. The Dunkeld Dynasty goes back to 1034 and prior was the Alpin Dynasty. Malcom's wife, St. Margaret the Exiled was daughter of an exiled prince of England, Edward the Exiled son of King Edmund II Ironside in the first restored House of Wessex.

Matilda, wife of William the Conqueror was of Royal lines. She had richer bloodlines than William and refused marriage to him at first. The other thing was that they were only 3 generations removed from relations and standard by law was 7 but when you're royalty, law doesn't apply. Her bloodlines are one of many in Lydia's family tree which traces back to the Capetians, this time through the Franks and also to Rollo, the Viking who conquered Normandy.

William himself, goes back to the House of Alpin as well as Rollo. Between Rollo and himself marriages tied the family tree to the Carolingian Dynasty. The Carolingians married into the Neustrian Dynasty and prior. Norman, Scoti, Frank and Saxon Royalty all intermarried. If they did not cover a part of Europe, the Capetians do with Capetians still in Royalty in Spain. Royalty married royalty to keep bloodlines pure.

Ephraim Allen 1691-1776 husband of Susannah Beacon has a strong heritage as well. Ephraim Sr. 1679-1727 was son of Samuel Allen 1658-1720 and Jane Ross 1664-1702. Jane was the daughter of James Ross 1635-1690, son of John Ross 1602-1643, son of Gilbert Ross 1575-1637. Gilbert is the son of James Ross and Jonet (Jean) Semple. The birth years for both

James and Jonet are a bit murky and there is not a lot of information but Jonet was the daughter of Lord Robert 3rd Lord Semphill/Semple 1505-1576, son of Lord William Semple 1485-1552 and Margaret Montgomery 1485-1523. Margaret was the daughter of Sir Hugh Montgomery Baron of Eglinton 1459-1545 son of Alexander Montgomery III 1436-1468 and Catherine Kennedy 1441-1533. Catherine Kennedy was the daughter Gilbert Kennedy 1405-1489 son of James Kennedy 1376-1408 husband to Mary Stewart 1380-1458. She was daughter to Robert Stewart III king of Scotland.

Back to Susannah Bacon who is the daughter of John Bacon 1670-1713. John is the son of John Bacon 1647-1723 and Susannah Draper 1650-1678. Susannah Draper is the daughter of James Draper 1622-1697 and Miriam Stanfield.

There are many variations of spelling for Stanfield. Prior to Miriam it is predominantly Standesfield. In the Stadesfield branch, Miriam was the daughter of Gideon 1601-1658, son of Abraham 1562-1642,son of Lawrence 1540-1591, son of

Thomas 1518-1565, son of Laurence 1478-1534, son of James 1450-1501 son of William 1438-, son of Thomas 1400-, son of John 1390-1457 husband of Lady Mary Fleming. The Standesfield family goes back more generations but for this study it stops where the Flemings marry in.

The Fleming line is very important, as they were the founding family of the Flemish part of the Netherlands. Mary was the daughter of John 1355-1415, son of William 1326-1386, Malcom 1312-1382, son of Patrick 1286-1320 and Joanna Fraser 1290-1312, Patrick being the son of Robert 1252-1314 and Joan Douglas Lady Fleming 1258-1307. Beyond Robert it goes back to Baldwin the Biggar.

Joanna Fraser 1290 was the daughter of Simon Fraser 1257-1306. Scott Fraser was a knight with much land. He fought for Scottish Independence alongside Andrew Moray and William Wallace. He fought alongside William Wallace when defeated at Happrew. He fought again under King Robert when he was defeated. He escaped and was captured at a subsequent battle, brought to London, hanged, drawn and quartered when Joanna was only 16.
Simon Married Lady Mary Bisset/Biset of Oliver. She was the daughter of John Bisset III Lord Lovat 1230-1268, son of John II 1190-1259 son of John I 1164-.

John I married Princess Leona Fitzwilliam 1162-1262. Fitzwilliam means son of and history is not clear whom she is a daughter of other than William De Warren but somewhere in the line of William the Lion King of Scotland. It's likely that she's the daughter of Gundred De Warren.[94] Whoever she's a daughter of is in dispute but that she's in the family is not in dispute. de Warren from before Gundred is the House of Dunkeld and beyond to the House of Alpin which was seen down the previous family branch. Following the de Warren line through Ada 1117-1178 her grandmother on her father's side is Gundred de St.Olmers who is said to be a disputed illegitimate child of William Beauclerc. She was born circa 1050. The fact that she was able to marry into nobility gives something to the fact that she might be William's daughter. On Ada's mother's side, her grandparents are Capetians again solidifying the nobility.

There are not a lot of records about John Bartholomew himself. There are some early census records available for Unadilla. The older records are harder to follow because it shows the head of household only and tally other household

94 https://aprilsworld.com/OurFamilytree/individual.php?pid=P2838&ged=tree3

members by gender and age. It creates a difficulty because there are no family member to compare to verify the authenticity of the record to the person listed nor is age listed. However, listed on the same sheets on each census record, Samuel, his father, is listed, as well as Levi, his brother. Levi is the one who wrote the letter on behalf of Samuel for his pension.

The census also shows occupations, which for John it has him listed as a basket maker through the 1855 New York State Census. In 1860 he was listed as the farmer, which was the occupation of both his father and his brother Levi and possibly his brother, Samuel. The farm was in the family at least two more generation.

Below is an image of an affidavit John Bartholomew did on behalf of his father's pension. The importance of this is it does have John's actually signature.

State of New-York, } ss. John Bartholomew of the
OTSEGO COUNTY, } town of Unadilla in the County
aforesaid ——— being duly sworn, saith, that he is personally well
acquainted with Samuel Bartholomew the applicant above
named, and has been so acquainted with him the said Samuel Bartholomew
for twenty years, and during that time the said Samuel
Bartholomew has sustained a good character for truth and veracity, and he this deponent verily believes that full credit ought to be given to the declarations of the said Samuel Bartholomew when under oath.
and further the Deponent saith that he well knows
the said Samuel Bartholomew to be Infirm and
Indigent and that he is absolutely in Need of the
assistance of his Country for support
John Bartholomew

United States Census, 1820

Moses B Maxwell	2	
John B Buckley	3	
Simeon Palmer	2	
Charles Brooks	3	
Robert Day	1	1
John Brooks	1	
Samuel Bartholomew		
John Bartholomew	2	
John Hains	1	1
Jabish Maynard	2	
Joseph Smith		
Luther De Forest	1	
Samuel Smith	3	1
William Carr	1	

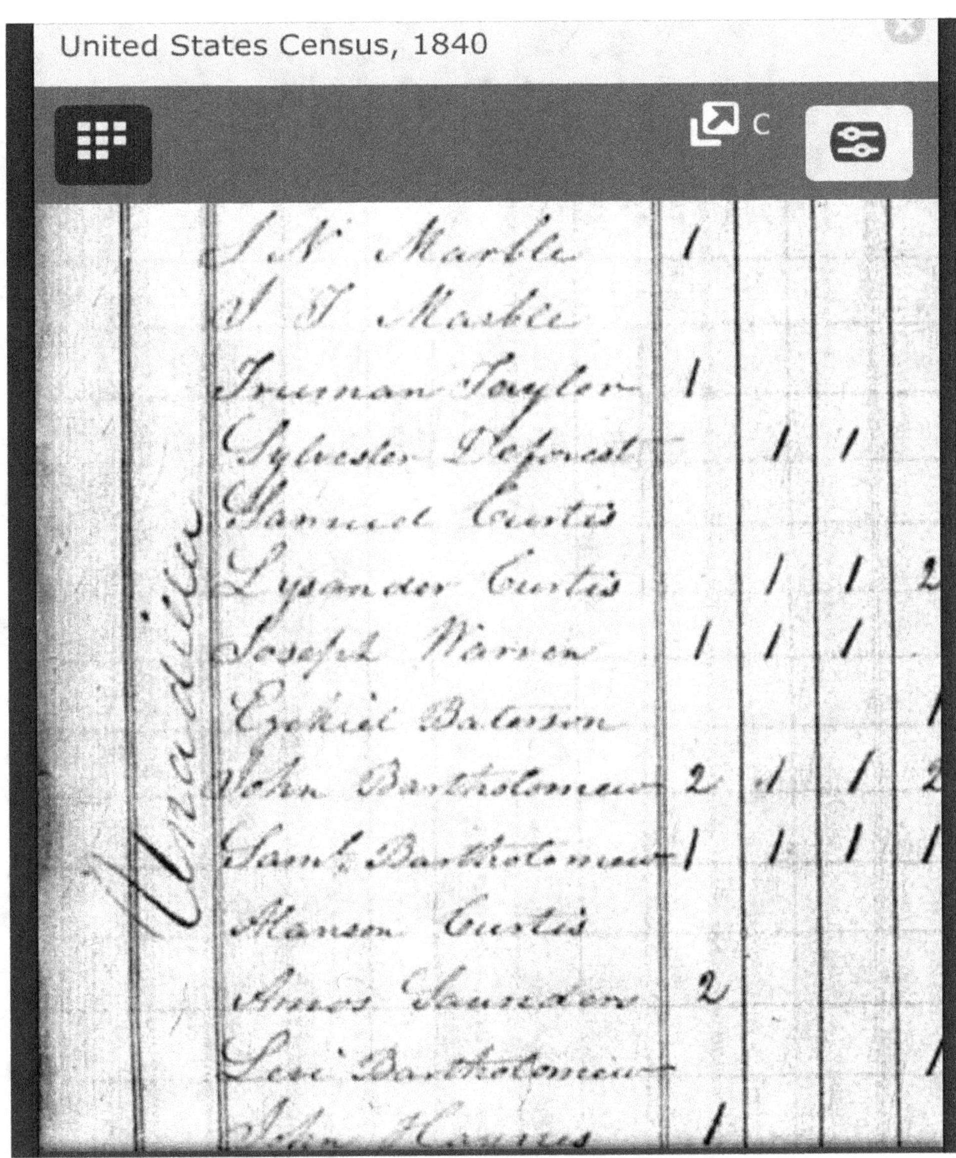

The next two are the 1855 census, the second with a

closer view. Line 11 shows John.

SCHEDULE I.—Free Inhabitants in [illegible] **in the County of** [illegible] **State of** [illegible] **enumerated by me, on the** [illegible] **day of** [illegible] **1850.** [illegible] **Ass't Marshal.**

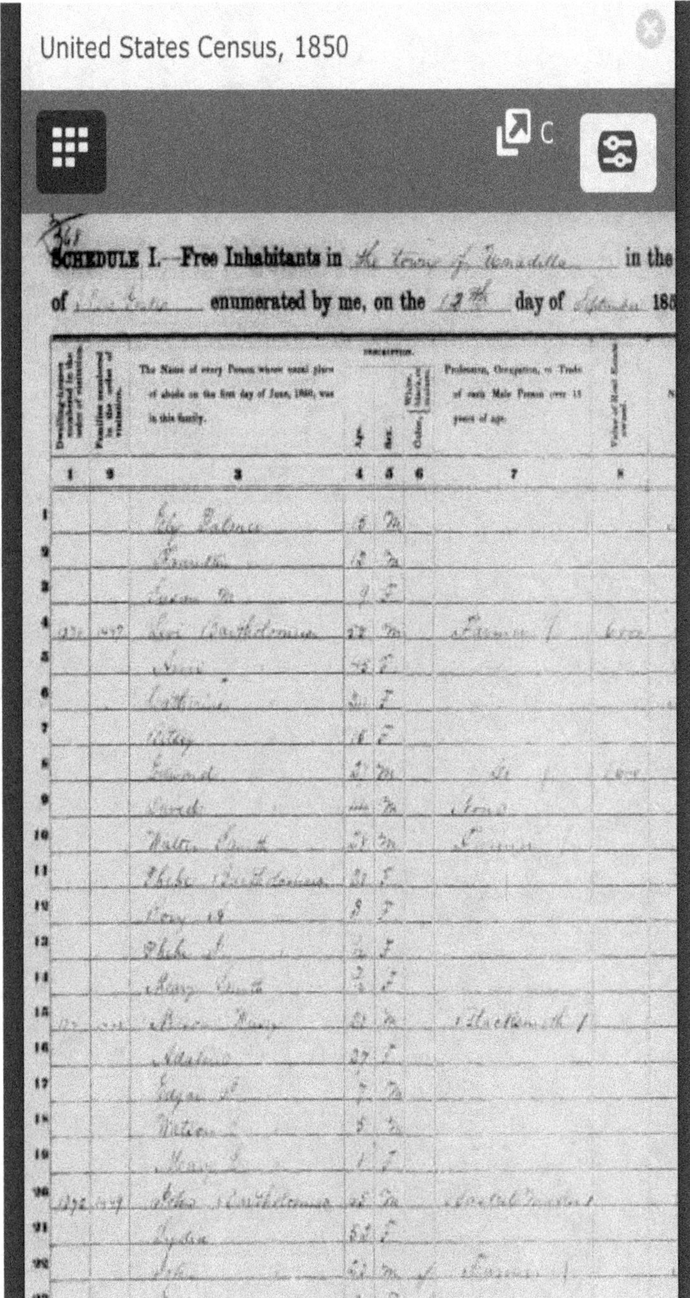
United States Census, 1850

SCHEDULE I.—Free Inhabitants in the town of Unadilla in the

of ... enumerated by me, on the 12th day of September 185

Caleb Bartholomew

I. Population. CENSUS of the Inhabitants in the [illegible] Election District of the [illegible] [illegible] in the County of [illegible] taken by me on the 28th day of June, 1855.

[illegible]

	Dwellings numbered in the order of visitation	Of what material built	Value	Families numbered in the order of their visitation	Name of every person whose usual place of abode on the first day of June was in this family	Age	Sex	Color	Relation to the head of the family	In what county of this State, or in what other State or Foreign Country born	Married	Widowed	Years resident in this city or town	Profession, Trade, or Occupation	Voters: Native	Voters: Naturalized	Aliens	Persons of color not taxed	Persons over 21 years who cannot read and write
	1	2	3	4	5	6	7	8	9	10	11	12	13	14	15	16	17	18	19
1	[illegible]	[illegible]	250	[illegible]	Stephen [illegible]	64	m			[illegible]	1		36	[illegible]	1				
2					[illegible] do	56	f	[illegible]		do do	1		36						
3					[illegible] do	24	m	[illegible]		[illegible]			[illegible]		1				
4					[illegible] do	16	f	[illegible]		do			16						
5	[illegible]	[illegible]	150	[illegible]	[illegible]	63	f			[illegible]			26						
6					[illegible] do	[illegible]	f			do do			26						
7	[illegible]	[illegible]	200	[illegible]	[illegible]	31	m			[illegible]			31	[illegible]	1				
8					[illegible]	[illegible]	f	[illegible]		do			[illegible]						
9	[illegible]	[illegible]	70	[illegible]	John [illegible]	27	m			do	1		[illegible]		1				
10					[illegible] do	21	f	Wife		[illegible]	1		[illegible]						
11	[illegible]	[illegible]	70	[illegible]	[illegible] Bartholomew	63	m			State of Ct	1		[illegible]	[illegible]	1				
12					[illegible] do	57	f	[illegible]		do do	1		[illegible]						
13					[illegible] do	20	m	[illegible]		[illegible]			20						
14					[illegible] do	18	m	do		do			[illegible]						
15					[illegible] do	15	m	do		do			[illegible]						
16	[illegible]	[illegible]	[illegible]	[illegible]	[illegible]	73	m			[illegible]	1		[illegible]		1				
17					[illegible] do	60	f	[illegible]		[illegible]	1		[illegible]						
18					[illegible] do	[illegible]	m	[illegible]		[illegible]			[illegible]		1				
19	[illegible]	[illegible]	[illegible]	[illegible]	[illegible]	32	m			do	1		[illegible]	[illegible]	1				
20					[illegible] do	[illegible]	f	[illegible]		[illegible]	1		[illegible]						
21					[illegible] do	7	f	[illegible]		[illegible]			[illegible]						
22					[illegible] do	3	f	[illegible]		do			[illegible]						
23					[illegible]	[illegible]	f			[illegible]			[illegible]						
24	[illegible]	[illegible]	150	[illegible]	[illegible]	33	m			[illegible]	1		6	[illegible]	1				
25					[illegible] do	29	f	[illegible]		do	1		6						
26					[illegible] do	3	f	[illegible]		do			[illegible]						
27	[illegible]	[illegible]	[illegible]	[illegible]	[illegible]	66	m			State of Ct	1		28	[illegible]	1				
28					[illegible] do	[illegible]	f	[illegible]		do do	1		28						
29					[illegible] do	26	m	[illegible]		do do			28	[illegible]	1				
30					Charles do	21	m	do		do do			[illegible]		1				
31					Charlotte do	18	f	[illegible]		[illegible]			18						
32					[illegible] do	16	f	do		do			16						
33	[illegible]	[illegible]	[illegible]	[illegible]	[illegible] Palmer	62	m			[illegible]	1		36	[illegible]	1				
34					[illegible] do	59	f	[illegible]		do do	1		36						
35					Franklin do	17	m	[illegible]		[illegible]			17						
36					[illegible] do	15	f	[illegible]		do			[illegible]						
37	[illegible]	[illegible]	400	[illegible]	[illegible]	[illegible]	m			do	1		[illegible]	[illegible]	1				
38					[illegible] do	[illegible]	f	[illegible]		[illegible]	1		19						

I. Population. CENSUS of the Inhabitan

Unadilla in the County of Otsego

	Dwellings numbered in the order of visitation.	Of what material built.	Value.	Families numbered in the order of their visitation.	Name of every person whose usual place of abode on the first day of June was in this family.	Age.
	1	2	3	4	5	6
1	85	frame	250	85	Stephen Palmer	60
2					Sally do	56
3					Calvin do	24
4					Sally A do	16
5	86	frame	150	86	Betsy Palmer	63
6					Susan do	72
7	87	frame	200	87	Frederick Bartholomew	31
8					Hannah Tayler	38
9	88	frame	70	88	John Bartholomew	27
10					Elsie do	21
11	89	frame	70	89	John Bartholomew	68
12					Lydia do	57
13					Andrew do	20
14					[illegible] do	18

This shows John as a basket maker.

New York State Census, 1855

26				
36				
31	Shoe Mak.	1		
38				
27		1		
2/12				
50	Basket Mak.	1		
40				
20				

United States Census, 1860

C

223	223	Harry Potter	62	M	Farmer
		Mary "	62	F	
		Duane "	21	M	Farm Laborer
		Juliett "	19	F	
		Mariah Potter	18	F	Domestic
224	224	James Bartholomew	24	M	Farmer
		Aleha "	24	F	
		Abner Johnson	13	M	
225	225	Wheeler Warriner	70	M	Farmer
		Samantha "	62	F	
		Liman "	37	M	Mst Mason
		Teresa "	25	F	
		Mary Warriner	92	F	
226	226	Wm Vanaulstine	34	M	Farmer
		Ellen "	29	F	
		Philetus "	3/12	M	
		Clarissa Odell	21	F	Domestic
227	227	J D Bartholemew	36	M	Farmer
228	228	John Bartholomew	75	M	Farmer
		Lydia "	62	F	
		Andrew "	25	M	Farm Laborer
		[illegible] "	19	M	

Caleb Bartholomew

LYDIA
JOHN BARTHOLOMEW

Chapter 10 Chauncey Bartholomew 1816-?

366 Chauncey[7] (*John*[6], *Samuel*[5], *Samuel*[4],) born 23

Feb., 1816; married, second, Rebecca Locke; no issue; and third, Mrs. Sarah ——, by whom he had one son Angelo.

He resides in Sidney Plains, Delaware Co., N. Y.

Children:

523a i Charles A.,[8] b. 3 Aug., 1842; res. W. Onconta, N. Y.
ii Alfred C., b. 5 Feb., 1844; enlisted in the 121st N. Y. V. I. and was killed 10 May, 1864, in the battle of the wilderness.
iii Angelo.

As a contemporary of George Wells Bartholomew, there is little information concerning Chauncey Bartholomew. He does give us a date of birth, his children's names and the names of two of his wives.

This provided enough information to fill in some gaps. The first is it helps identify sources that bring us the name of his first wife as well as additional children.

Also what George Wells gives helps us find information leading to the oldest sons.

Charles A. served in the Union Army as well as Alfred C. Both sons had opposite experiences in the army. Alfred was killed and Charles A. never missed any time for anything as simple as an injury or the common cold.

Both military unit are easily traceable and give us a

much larger insight into their lives. As uncles to Frank Bartholomew their lives seem a little more interesting to this study. Because Alfred was killed, it is important to this author to let his legacy live on, as there are no known descendants of his. An appendix will be made to both of Frank's uncles. There service to the United States is impeccable. Alfred served at Gettysburg before his death and in many other battles. There are intricate writings about the battle that took his life and there are conflicting reports as to specifically which battle he died in but the two battles are within days of each other. Based on muster roles, it is likely that he did not die in the Battle of the Wilderness. There are also reports of him being missing in action and no body had ever been recovered. The intensity of the battle it is safe to assume he had died in the battle.

The details about Charles are also very easy to trace. He served in the artillery division. The number of battles he served in and where he served are also very detailed.

As to Chauncey, his first wife was Catherine Vandenburg. She was born in 1822 and likely died between 1850 and 1855. She is not listed in George Wells book but she is implied. She is the mother of Alfred and Charles. This can all be known from the 1850 census.

A child named Mary does not show up in any other census reports after the 1855 New York State Census. She is known as Mary Bartholomew on the 1855 Census but she is not present on the 1850 US Census, which means she may be the daughter of the second wife, Rebecca Locke who is also on the 1855 census. It is not known if Locke is her mother's maiden name, or married name meaning Mary's maiden name could be Locke. There is Mary Locke's who were born around the same time on an 1865 census with the mother with the same first initial and Locke as a last name who would have also been born around the same time but there is not enough information about either to make a connection. There is also a passenger list of immigrants from England that has Mrs. Locke (that's how it's listed) the same age and Mary Locke the same age, with other children also listed as children of said Mrs. Locke. But again there is not enough information to make a connection.

Rebecca Locke was his second wife. She is on the 1855 New York State census and also 1860 US Census. Chauncey had no children with her from every record including George Wells. There is no known record for a marriage date for either of the first two marriages or for the third. There is no record of what happened to either of the first two, whether deceased or whether divorced. Even though they had no children together it is likely Mary was her child. Mary, however, is not on the 1860 census and her status is unknown after that.

On the 1865 New York State Census, only one son is on

the census as an adult and a farmhand or servant. One son was killed in the war, one son returned from the war and Angelo wasn't born yet.

The third marriage, Sarah Jaycox is the mother of Angelo. She likely had a child in a previous marriage. Her tombstone is known and she was buried under her first husband's last name. After Angelo was born, her and her first son are on other census records together, apart from Chauncey and Angelo under her previous married name so it is likely that they got divorced. She had gone back to live with her first husband's family which means he likely deceased before she married Chauncey.

Angelo was born in 1867 after the Civil War had ended. He and Sarah do not show up on the next census record we have which is the 1875 census. Chauncey's relation to the head of the household is alone. He is still listed as a farmer at this time.

Chauncey's date of death or place of burial is not known. Unlike everyone else in the family tree we have a date range for death and or a reason for death. There is none for Chauncey. Some people speculate that he died shortly after the 1875 census but he does appear on the 1880 US Census as widowed and possibly living with Charles, his wife Jeanie and their daughter Jennie. Both Charles and Chauncey are listed as farmers on that census. Many historians have given Chauncey a date of death though none is known. No search has turned up with his name attached to a grave. Charles was buried in a different part of the state as well as Angelo and no name matches Chauncey Bartholomew in those cemeteries. Many of his siblings were buried near their parents in the same cemetery and others in the surrounding cemeteries in Otsego County.

Sarah Jaycox family tree is not as rich as Lydia Maynard's but it is deep and has some strong names in it.

One name as a distance cousin is Jasper Tudor who was the illegitimate son of Henry VII. Jasper's daughter Helen married a Gardiner. Sarah's 3rd great grandfather on her grandmother's side married a Gardiner. The Gardiner family settled in Narraganset, Rhode Island with a book of their family history written.[95] Her 3rd great grandfather was Caleb Hazard 1697-1726 and 3rd great grandmother Abigail Gardiner 1700-1772. Two generations before the Gardiner's migrated to the America's Henry Gardiner married Mary Howard. Mary Howard is a descendant of Robert Howard and Margaret de Mowbray. Her grandmother was Elizabeth de Badlesmere Bohun daughter of Margaret de Clare granddaughter to Edward Longshanks. The Howard line is the same Howard who was the Uncle to Elizabeth Howard and Anne Boleyn. This was Thomas Howard III Duke of

[95] The book is literally "The Gardiner's of Narraganset"1914

Norfolk. This connection has not been 100% verified. It is more likely than not that this is the family but without a certain connection being made the connections would be based on probability and not certainty.

From Sarah Jaycox, her father William 1798-, his father John 1770-1857 who married Sarah Hazard 1773-1836, daughter of Edward 1753-1778, son of William 1721-, son of Caleb 1697-1726 who married Abigail Gardiner 1700-1772, daughter of William 1671-1732, son of Benoni 1636-1729, son of George the America patriarch 1599-1677, son of Rev. Michael 1552-1630, son of Henry 1500-1564 who married Mary Howard 1528-1580 daughter of Michael Howard: we get the line to possibly reach the Howard family in question. Some sources again say his father was John Howard 1482-1523 who was the son of Thomas III Duke of Norfolk. John was not the heir apparent and there is little information on him and it is possible that his son who would be less known because he is also not heir apparent would be Michael. Further research would have to be given to find the connection 100%.

One name that is for certain is the Arnold name. This name can be traced back to the colonial governor of Rhode Island, Benedict Arnold, 2nd great grandfather to the general at West Point who tried to sell the fort to the British as American history would tell it.

Caleb Hazard's maternal great grandfather was

Governor Arnold. His mother was Penelope 1669-1742, his grandfather was Capt. Caleb Arnold 1644-1719 and his great grandfather was Gov. Benedict Arnold 1615-1678.

44

SCHEDULE I.—Free Inhabitants in Walton **in the County of** Delaware **State of** New York **enumerated by me, on the** 6th **day of** Sept **1850.** [illegible] **Ass't Marshal**

	Dwelling-houses numbered in the order of visitation.	Families numbered in the order of visitation.	The Name of every Person whose usual place of abode on the first day of June, 1850, was in this family.	Age	Sex	Color	Profession, Occupation, or Trade of each Male Person over 15 years of age.	Value of Real Estate owned.	Place of Birth. Naming the State, Territory, or Country.	Married within the year.	Attended School within the year.	Persons over 20 y'rs of age who cannot read & write.	Whether deaf and dumb, blind, insane, idiotic, pauper, or convict.
	1	2	3	4	5	6	7	8	9	10	11	12	13
1			Geo. Alverson	23	m		Farmer	3000	N.Y.				
2	[illegible]	[illegible]	Elizabeth [illegible] "	57	f				ct				
3			Frances C "	28	f				N.Y.				
4			Mary A "	21	f				"				
5			Lafayette Fitch	12	m				"		1		
6	243	268	Anson Alverson	32	m		Farmer	1500	"				
7			Deborah "	31	f				"				
8			Ruth A "	10	f				"		1		
9			Wm Otis "	7	m				"		1		
10			Julia ma "	1	f				"				
11	[illegible]	[illegible]	Chauncy Bartholomew	33	m		Farmer	150	"				
12			Catharine "	40	f				"				
13			C Albert "	7	m				"		1		
14			Alfred "	7	m				"		1		

Page No. 21 — 337

SCHEDULE 1.—Free Inhabitants in Unadilla **in the County of** Otsego **State of** N York **enumerated by me, on the** 19th **day of** June **1860.** W. F. Edson **Ass't Marshal**

Post Office Unadilla

	Dwelling-houses numbered in the order of visitation.	Families numbered in the order of visitation.	The name of every person whose usual place of abode on the first day of June, 1860, was in this family.	Age	Sex	Color	Profession, Occupation, or Trade of each person, male and female, over 15 years of age.	Value of Real Estate	Value of Personal Estate	Place of Birth, Naming the State, Territory, or Country.	Married within the year.	Attended School within the year.	Persons over 20 y'rs of age who cannot read & write.	Whether deaf and dumb, blind, insane, idiotic, pauper, or convict.	
	1	2	3	4	5	6	7	8	9	10	11	12	13	14	
1	169	169	Chancy Bartholomew	45	M		Farmer Lab.	240	80	NY					1
2			Releca "	48	F					"					2
3			Charles "	18	M		" "			"		1			3
4			Alfred "	17	M					Pa		1			4
5	170	170	James Mitcalf	36	M		Farmer	1500	100	Ny					5
6			Martha "	27	F					"					6

I. Population. CENSUS of the Inhabitants in the Second Election District of the Town Tompkins in the County of Delaware taken by me on the 2d day of ~~June~~ July, 1855.

E. C. Adams

Dwelling No.	Of what material built	Value	Families No.	Name	Age	Sex	Relation to head of family	Birthplace	Married	Widowed	Years resident	Profession, Trade, or Occupation	Native voters
247	Plank	700	262	Joseph Wakeman	27	M		Delaware	1		27	Farmer	1
				Washington Wakeman	20	M	Brother	Delaware			20	Farmer	
				Peter Wakeman	18	M	Brother	Delaware			18	Farmer	
				Alonzo Wakeman	17	M	Brother	Delaware			17	Farmer	
248	Plank	150	263	Francis W. Frazier	38	M		Delaware	1		38	Farmer	1
				Julia A. Frazier	33	F	Wife	Delaware	1		33		
				Arad Frazier	12	M	Son	Delaware			12		
				Clark Frazier	5	M	Son	Delaware			5		
249	Frame	100	264	John Alverson	76	M		Nova Scotia	1		40	Farmer	1
				Jane Alverson	68	F	Wife	Nova Scotia	1		40		
250	Frame	400	265	John Alverson Jr	41	M		Delaware	1		41	Farmer	1
				Mary A. Alverson	33	F	Wife	Delaware	1		33		
				Alice Alverson	11	F	Daughter	Delaware			11		
				Ellen J. Alverson	8	F	Daughter	Delaware			8		
251	Frame	350	266	Daniel Alverson	37	M		Delaware	1		37	Farmer	1
				Ann E. Alverson	33	F	Wife	Delaware	1		33		
				Charles Alverson	8	M	Son	Delaware			8		
				Deloy Alverson	4	M	Son	Delaware			4		
				Esther Alverson	1	F	Daughter	Delaware			1		
252	Plank	40	267	Chauncey Bartholomew	38	M		Otsego	1		6	Farmer	1
				Rebecca Bartholomew	38	F	Wife	Schoharie	1		6		
				Charles Bartholomew	12	M	Son	Otsego			6		
				Alfred Bartholomew	10	M	Son	Penn			6		
				Mary Bartholomew	8	F	Daughter	Otsego			6		

I. Population. CENSUS of the Inhabitants living in the 2nd Election District of the Town Page 7

of Unadilla in the County of Otsego, N. Y., on the first day of June, 1865.

This Enumeration was made by me, on the tenth day of June, 1865.

(2.)

Enumerator.

311

SCHEDULE 1.—Inhabitants in ______, in the County of ______, State of ______

enumerated by me on the ______ day of June, 1880.

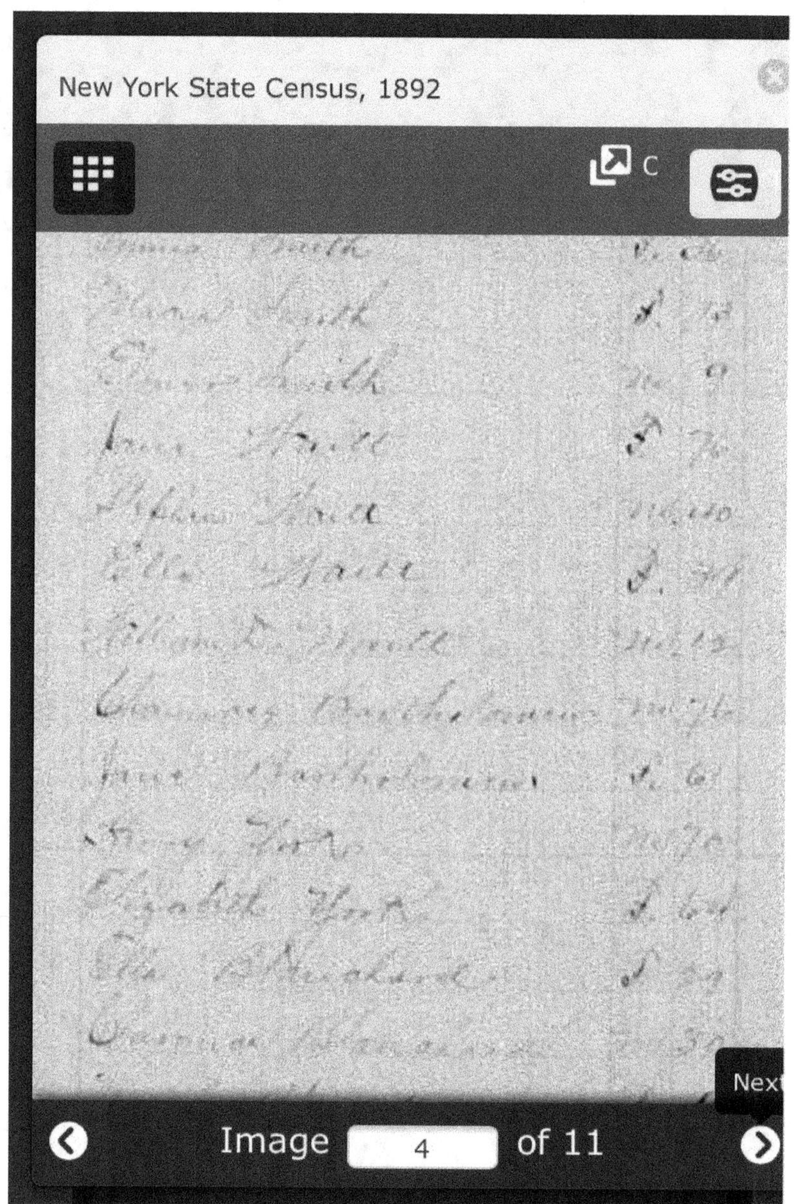
New York State Census, 1892
Next
Image 4 of 11

Unadilla Center, Otsego Co., N.Y.
Part of the farmland once owned by Samuel Bartholomew,
This was part of a rock fence built from rocks cleared from fields. Chauncey Bartholomew, Dan's brother lived near this fence in Delaware County, N.Y. about 1860. His home was a log home, Dan and Minerva lived in a nearby village where he taught school.

Chapter 11 Angelo Jaycox Bartholomew 1867-1936

Angelo was born in 1867, a couple years after the end of the civil war. Angelo is on the census with Chauncey early on in his life, with his mother, Sarah Jaycox. George Wells mentions Angelo living in Delaware County in his book with use of the present tense, as he was a contemporary of Angelo. Sarah Jaycox is mentioned but her offspring is not mentioned from a previous marriage and it does not mention her as residing in Delaware County almost as though she is past tense. The public documents that lead us to his connection with our family tree is on his second marriage certificate, Sarah is mentioned as his mother and Chauncey as his father. Eyewitnesses to his second wife confirm this as well. Grandchildren of Angelo have met and talked to Agnes Duryea, Angelo's second wife.

Angelo's first wife was Lena Follette. Some family records show Lena's last name as La Follette. This will be covered more below.

The first census Angelo would have been was the 1870 when he was three years old. It shows him with Chauncey, his father, Sarah, his mother and James Darroch, Angelo's half brother, from Sarah's previous marriage. James is important Angelo's history. This is the only census Angelo is on with his father. Both are alive for at least 15 more years. This trend of multiple marriages with children only being in one parent's home continued for a few more generations fairly similar to Angelo's experience. Nothing indicates that Angelo was not around Chauncey at all he's just not listed on US or state census reports. George Wells says Angelo is living with Chauncey in Sidney Plaines. The book was published in 1896 but the depth and breadth of George's study there is no way to know when Angelo lived there. Chauncey is not reported in any census as living in Sidney Plaines. He did move a bit so it could be in between any census or beyond the last census for Chauncey. Because Angelo and Chauncey were contemporary to George we know this is accurate information even without any other supporting information.

Angelo appears in every census while he's alive which is helpful for additional information and making conclusions to his life. The next census he's in is 1875.

In 1875 he's with his mother, but they are in the household of James Darroch. James, who was listed as a farmhand, at age 16, in 1870, is now listed as the head of household. He was 21 by the time the 1875 census came around. They were in the town of Morris in Otsego County and James occupation was listed as a farmer. Angelo would have been 8 at this time. Sarah kept the surname Bartholomew at this time as well. Chauncey was in Unadilla on the same census.

On the 1880 census Angelo still lived in Morris. He is listed as a farm laborer at the age of 13. This census also asks if he's in school and he's not listed as being in school. Sarah's surname is now camp and they are either living with James still or next door to James who is now 26 and married.

One take away from him being a laborer at 13 is We don't know exactly when he started as a farm laborer but he had been for awhile. Not living with his father, he was forced to grow up too young. His grandson, Richard Bartholomew recounts Frank Bartholomew's assessment of Angelo as an adult. Frank and his sister Mae were not allowed to go out and play with other children even though they themselves were children. They weren't doing anything else but they could hear other children laughing and playing outside and on occasion could see them sledding on a nearby hill even. It is curious to know if this was a result of Angelo having no childhood. If he couldn't play as a child why should any child play? Perhaps children are not supposed to play in his perception. Perhaps it made him feel like he turned out better because of it and what parent would not their children to be the best.

The 1892 census is quite interesting. New York from 1825-1875 did a census every 10 years. In 1892 the courthouses held a statewide census and kept their own records of it. This is very helpful historically because the US Census in 1890 was lost in a fire in 1921. For New Yorkers' the gap of information is not as wide as other states since they did a census off cycle. The next state census was not taken in 1905[96]. It's not known also why there was no census in 1885 by the state.

On the 1892 census, Angelo is in Unadilla again. There is 12 years between existing census records so it is unknown how long he was in Unadilla. It could be that he was living in Sidney with Chauncey during that stretch and many of those years he would have been a minor. His occupation listed on this census is laborer but many of the jobs it appears were farmer or laborer so he would have likely still be an a farm laborer. Frank Bartholomew told of memories of farm life so it is likely that the labor work was done.

In researching the 1892 census, the author realized there were only 12 pages to the Unadilla Census. One page before was Chauncey Bartholomew, farmer, same age, and same residence. This finding is interesting due to the fact that this is much older than anyone else had Chauncey. He's 76. He's also living with who looks like Jane Bartholomew

---

[96] http://search.ancestry.com/search/db.aspx?dbid=3212
New York State Library
Ancestry.com. *New York, State Census, 1892* [database on-line]. Provo, UT, USA: Ancestry.com Operations, Inc., 2012.
Original data: *1892 New York State Census.* New York State Education Department, Office of Cultural Education. New York State Library, Albany, NY.

born around 1830. The possibilities that it could be anyone other than a fourth wife are fairly slim. If Chauncey he a daughter at 16 she would have likely showed up on prior census data whether in John's household early on or at the least. It's less likely to be a sister since his siblings are already known and a sister born within the same year she was born.

Whoever she is, the importance is more to do with the fact that Angelo returned home to his father. Though in different homes, there were plenty of other places to side in Otsego County and even more outside. Sarah and James Darroch are both alive still and James still a farmer. It is curious to know what happened between Sarah and Chauncey and how it affected Angelo. Whatever happened it seems Angelo gravitated back to where his father was.

The next record does not come for eight more years. The industrial revolution was in full swing but the sleepy little farming communities kept their task of feeding those who worked in factories and mines.

In the 1900 census, Angelo is in New Berlin, New York. He is married and has a daughter and a baby on the way. New Berlin is only 25 miles away from both Sidney and Morris where Angelo had also lived. Without the invention of the automobile, New Berlin was a day's travel away by foot in today's condition.

Lena Follette is Angelo's wife on the census. The Follette lineage can be traced back to England to the 15th century with as much certainty as the Bartholomew line.

Angelo was 33 at the time and Lena was 22. Their daughter May (Mae) was 2. This census also reveals that Angelo and Lena were married for 5 years at the time. It asks how many children Lena had and how many were still living and she answered one for both.

Angelo, while he was reported to live on a farm per family history, is listed as a painter on the census. The farm could have been what we call a hobby farm now or just enough to feed the family or it could have been on functional. The census lists that this is a house as opposed to a farm, however, and it shows it as a rental.

In 1910 Angelo has moved to Syracuse, New York. He's listed as a widower though other information shows that isn't true. He is a boarder in Syracuse but maintains the same title as a painter and his work is interior painting. The 1910 census asked if he had work every month in 1910 and he answered yes. It asked if he had work every month in 1909 to which he also answered yes. There is no indication how long he had lived in Syracuse up until this time. It is not known why he was in Syracuse but it's a 90-minute drive in today's roads. It would have been a full 24-hour walk. Transportation was changing at the time so he could have driving or caught a ride at least for part of the trip.

The next historical evidence we have is a marriage license and a marriage certificate. The license has the address listed of the officiating person whose address is next to the Solvay, New York United Methodist Church. It doesn't give a venue for the marriage but it is likely to be there. Given his strictness, Methodism is a very likely match for s lifestyle match. Methodism is a system of methods for obtaining absolute holiness.

Both Angelo and Agnes are listed on the license. Angelo marked down that he was married and that it ended in 1908 from divorce. On the application, it asks if his first wife is dead and he says he thinks. It does state that his father is Chauncey Bartholomew and his mother is Sarah Jacox and his birthplace is Unadilla. Agnes reported on the 1910 census that she was a widow. Her marriage certificate Information Solvay is in the Syracuse community. Agnes lived in the area since 1905 so it's likely she's not the reason Angelo moved to Solvay. Prior to 1905 Agnes was in other areas of New York but originally from New Jersey.

The 1915 New York census is not available for print through current sources but the information on it is available. He is listed in Geddes, New York, which is in the same county as Syracuse. In the 1920 census, they are still in Geddes and Angelo is in the same line of work. The 1920 census goes into more detail as calling Angelo a decorator for homes. Decorators were what we call interior designers today.

Art Deco was what everything was decorated in at the time. The beginning of the Roaring 1920's is when this really caught on. It began more after World War I. Everything from interior design to exterior design to electronics were all done in Deco including the Empire State Building and Chrysler building. The opulence and luxury portrayed in the Great Gatsby was alive and well. Syracuse was not exempt as they still have buildings in their skyline that are Deco in style.[97]

By the 1930 census, things had changed. The Great Depression was in full swing. The first time in 30 years, Angelo was not a decorator or a painter. He was a high school janitor. Even if Agnes still had money, the people who were hiring decorators in the first third of the century were not anymore, at least not at a level to make a living on. Their residence was changed to Solvay when in1920 they were in Geddes, New York.

Anges' granddaughter is on this census. She could have come for a visit or perhaps it gave her daughter reprieve to have her granddaughter live there. Roberta Duryea was the granddaughter's name, from a child from Agnes's first marriage.

Angelo answered yes to being employed all months of 1929 so he was able to find employment without any issues after the stock market crashed. He also hadn't been unemployed any of 1930. Nothing on this census indicates anything about home ownership but the fact that they had to

---

[97] https://www.britannica.com/art/Art-Deco/images-videos

reside elsewhere and have their 16-year-old granddaughter with them is curious.

The move may be non-existent however, the village of Solvay is part of Geddes so depending on who does the census, and it maybe listed as either. The 1920 census does not show a district to show if a move had occurred. The address listed on the marriage certificate is now in the backyard of the current high school. The current yard in which the school is built is big enough that even if they rebuilt the high school since 1930 they could have done it on the same property. For Angelo to have worked at high school would make sense and it would make sense that they would still be living in the same home in 1930 as they were in 1911.

Angelo died on July 4, 1936 still living in Syracuse per FindAGrave.com He was 69 years old and he never made it out of the Great Depression and got back into decorating.

While family members who provided information for this book knew Agnes, the matriarch was Lena Follett. In Edith Raphael Bartholomew's Bible there were pages dedicated to a family tree. On those pages it had Lena's maiden name as La Follett and that's how the generation knew her. However, public records including marriage certificates, and census materials have her name as well as her ancestor's surname as Follett so the La was added in error by the subsequent generations. Lena's father was William Spencer Follett 1855-1923 and her mother was Alice Marie Dyer 1833-. William's father was Marshall Abraham Follett 1833-1907 and mother Susan A. Goodrich 1828-1918. The rest of the Follett male line is as follows:

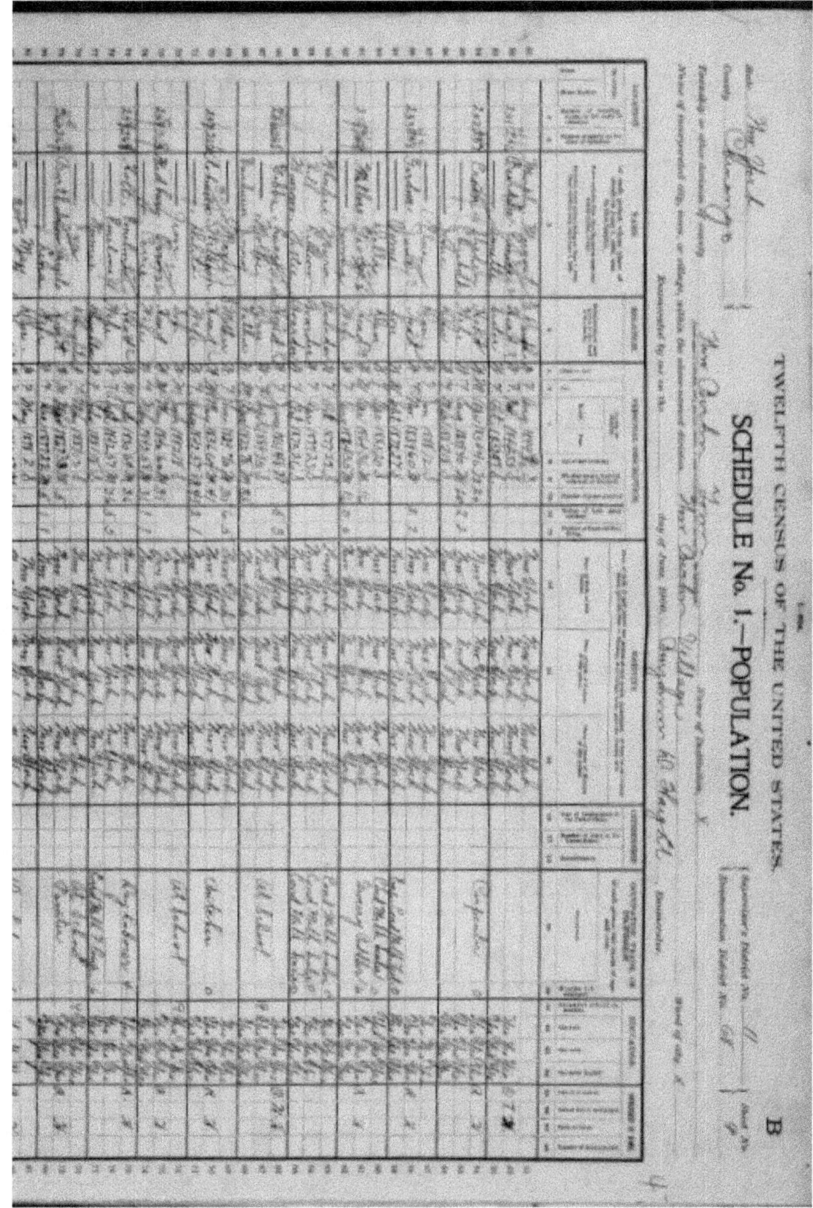

TWELFTH CENSUS OF THE UNITED STATES.

SCHEDULE No. 1.—POPULATION.

B

Samuel 1802-1885, Elijah 1775-1816, Robert 1739-1810, Robert 1712-1742, John 1669-1718, Robert 1672-1708, John 1605-1693 and Robert 1557-.

Page No. 1

Inquiries numbered 7, 16, and 17 are not to be asked in respect to infants. Inquiries numbered 11, 12, 15, 16, 17, 18, and 20 are to be answered (if at all) merely by an affirmative mark, as /.

SCHEDULE 1.—Inhabitants in [illegible], in the County of [illegible], State of [illegible], enumerated by me on the [illegible] day of [illegible], 1870. 282

Post Office: [illegible] B.H. Matteson, *Ass't Marshal.*

Below: same census zoomed in

		— Geo. W	3	M	W	
		— Wm	1	M	W	
6	6	Demming D. T.	50	M	W	Farmer
		— Caroline	28	F	W	keep house
7	7	Bartholomew Chas	44	M	W	Farmer
		— Sarah	38	F	W	keep house
		— Angelo	3	M	W	
		Darrach James	16	M	W	Farm

No. of dwellings, 7 No. of white females, 17 No. of males, foreign born,
" " families, 7 " " colored males, " " females, "
" " white males, 23 " " " females, " " blind,

Page No. 5
Supervisor's Dist. No. 5
Enumeration Dist. No. 107

235

SCHEDULE 1.—Inhabitants in Morris, in the County of Otsego, State of New York enumerated by me on the 3rd day of June, 1880.

Page

Enumeration of the Inhabitants living in the First Election District of the Town of [illegible], in the County of Otsego, N. Y., on Feb. 16, 1892.

Enumerator

NAME		NAME	

DEPARTMENT OF COMMERCE AND LABOR—BUREAU OF THE CENSUS

THIRTEENTH CENSUS OF THE UNITED STATES: 1910—POPULATION

9-18-09-100,000 (21-C-8788) 218

STATE OF NEW YORK

Affidavit for License to Marry

STATE OF NEW YORK
County of Onondaga
State of New York

Angelo J. Bartholomew and Agnes A. Duryea applicants for a license for marriage, being severally sworn, depose and say, that to the best of their knowledge and belief the following statement respectively signed by them is true, and that no legal impediment exists as to the right of the applicants to enter into the marriage state.

FROM THE GROOM:	FROM THE BRIDE:
Full name: Angelo J. Bartholomew	Full name: Agnes A. Duryea
Color: white	Color: white
Place of residence: 101 Sixth St, Solvay, N.Y.	Place of residence: 110 Lionel Ave, Solvay, N.Y.
Age: 44	Age: 49
Occupation: painter and paper hanger	Occupation: nurse
Place of birth: Unadilla, N.Y.	Place of birth: Boonton, N.J.
Name of father: Chancey Bartholomew	Name of father: David Taylor
Country of birth: Unadilla, N.Y.	Country of birth: Pumpton, N.J.
Maiden name of mother: Sara Jacox	Maiden name of mother: Charlott Bott
Country of birth: Morris, N.Y.	Country of birth: Towaca, N.J.
Number of marriage: second	Number of marriage: third
Former wife or wives living or dead: dead [illegible]	Former husband or husbands living or dead: dead
Is applicant a divorced person: yes	Is applicant a divorced person:
If so, when and where divorce or divorces were granted: Cooperstown, June, 1908	If so, when and where divorce or divorces were granted:

Angelo J. Bartholomew
GROOM

Agnes A. Duryea
BRIDE

Subscribed and sworn to before me this

29 day of Dec. 1911

W. Hoyt Foote
Clerk

T-16-09-100,000 (81-8086)

PLACE OF REGISTRY
County of Onondaga
City or Town of Geddes

NEW YORK STATE DEPARTMENT OF HEALTH
Bureau of Vital Statistics
CERTIFICATE AND RECORD OF MARRIAGE
Registered No. 218

Know all Men by this Certificate, that any person authorized by law to perform marriage ceremonies within the State of New York to whom this may come, he, not knowing any lawful impediment thereto, is hereby authorized and empowered to solemnize the rites of matrimony between Angelo J. Bartholomew of Solvay in the county of Onondaga and State of New York, and Agnes A. Duryea of Solvay in the county of Onondaga and State of New York and to certify the same to be said parties or either of them under his hand and seal in his ministerial or official capacity and thereupon he is required to return his certificate in the form hereto annexed.

In Testimony Whereof, I have hereunto set my hand and affixed the seal of said town or city at Solvay this 29 day of December one thousand nine hundred and eleven

W. Hoyt Smith
Town Clerk

{SEAL}

CLERK

I, Henry B. Allen, a minister residing at Solvay in the county of Onondaga and State of New York do hereby certify that I did on this 30th day of December in the year A. D. 1911 at Solvay in the county of Onondaga and State of New York solemnize the rites of matrimony between Angelo J. Bartholomew of Solvay in the county of Onondaga and State of New York and Agnes A. Duryea of Solvay in the county of Onondaga and State of New York in the presence of George W. Brown and Mrs. Mary C. Brown as witnesses and the license therefor is hereto annexed.

Witness my hand at Solvay in the county of Onondaga this 30th day of December A. D. 1911.

In the presence of
Geo W. Brown
Mary C. Brown
(Signatures of Witnesses)

Henry B. Allen
(Signature of Person performing Ceremony)
#204 Center St.
(Residence, Street and No.)

Angelo Bartholomew Photo Request
I located and photographed Angelo Bartholomew's stone in Myrtle Hill cemetery. His name is actually carved on the back of a stone for the Truax family. According to the interment books for this cemetery, he is buried directly in front of the eastern side of the stone, and his wife Alice is buried to his left, but there is no marker or any notation for her. I put some flowers in her location and took another photo; I can upload this to her memorial if you like. I did not see any other Bartholomews when I was there. MK

Added by MK on Aug 20, 2017 1:16 AM

DEPARTMENT OF COMMERCE—BUREAU OF THE CENSUS
FIFTEENTH CENSUS OF THE UNITED STATES: 1930
POPULATION SCHEDULE

DEPARTMENT OF COMMERCE—BUREAU OF THE CENSUS

FOURTEENTH CENSUS OF THE UNITED STATES: 1920—POPULATION

STATE · COUNTY · SUPERVISOR'S DISTRICT NO. · ENUMERATION DISTRICT NO. · SHEET NO. B

TOWNSHIP OR OTHER DIVISION OF COUNTY · NAME OF INCORPORATED PLACE · WARD OF CITY

NAME OF INSTITUTION · ENUMERATED BY ME ON THE ___ DAY OF January, 1920. ___ ENUMERATOR.

PLACE OF ABODE.	NAME	RELATION.	TENURE.	PERSONAL DESCRIPTION.	CITIZENSHIP.	EDUCATION.	NATIVITY AND MOTHER TONGUE.	OCCUPATION.

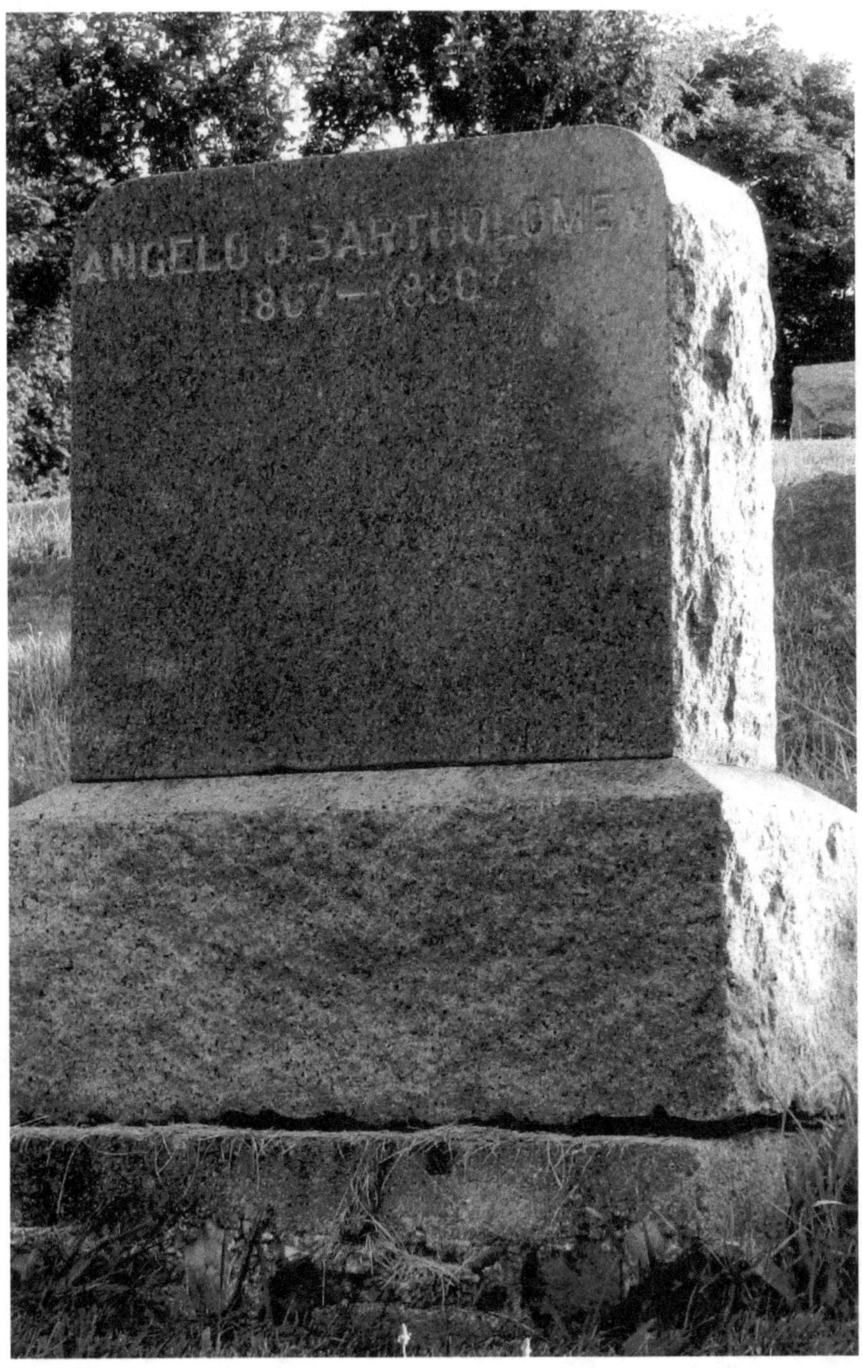
ANGELO J. BARTHOLOMEW

Chapter 12 Frank Bartholomew 1900-1968

Frank Bartholomew was born to Angelo Bartholomew and Lena Follette on October 12, 1900. He was born after the 1900 US census was taken which includes his parents and his sister Mae or Sarah May. As we read with Angelo, he had left the family and moved to Syracuse. It is unknown what prompted the divorce and relocation.

In 1905 the family was altogether still on the New York Census. Frank was 4 years old. His sister who was listed as Mae on the 1900 census is known as Sarah M on the 1905 census. At this time they were living in New Berlin, New York. Frank recounts times in their childhood hearing other children playing outside and not being able to go outside and play with them. They did not play inside either. They sat and listened to the laughter of the other children. It was with just a few short years later the children were left in an orphanage. Frank told his children that he had been in an orphanage in 1908. This is verified also through the 1910 census. On the census they along with many other children were listed as inmates who at the time could be children in an orphanage. Both Frank and Mae were inmates on this census. Per this census, it says the orphanage was located in Syracuse so it could be that the family had moved to Syracuse already before the divorce happened. In the same 1910 census, Angelo is listed as a boarder in a home with many other people also listed as boarders. Angelo could not have his children with him likely if he rented a single room.

The name of the orphanage was Onondaga Orphans' Home, which is listed on the top of the census. Onondaga Orphans' Home had fully functioning medical and dental facilities and was funded by solely by private donations. Onondaga, especially Syracuse, was very well known for its hospitals. For the time, it had a ton of medical facilities.

The fact that Syracuse was known for hospitals is curious because Frank had become deathly ill when he was 5 years old, shortly after the 1905 census. The thought today is that he had polio but nothing confirms that for sure. What is known is that Frank was deaf dumb and blind for a period of time from whatever disease vexed him. The doctor said the merciful thing for Frank would be if he just died. It's not known if those were New Berlin doctors who prompted a move to Syracuse or if his sickness already brought him to Syracuse because Otsego did not have the same kind of medical facilities and a Syracuse doctor said that. It is not known if the family relocated because of Frank's sickness but after 100+ years in New Berlin, something finally drew the family out. The need for medical attention and the medical help available in Syracuse would be motivation to make the move.

The disease left severe paralysis on Frank's right side of the body. His right hand was always shriveled and he walked with a pronounced limp. The disease probably stunted his growth, as he was 5 foot 9 inches tall if that, and a whopping 145 as an adult.[98]

Frank was listed as a child of Angelo and Agnes on the 1915 census, in Geddes, New York. This is important because it shows Angelo recovered his children out of the orphanage.

Frank blamed Angelo for abandoning him at Mae at the orphanage and never forgave him. He was reported having always said that since he was in his twenties he wanted to give Angelo a piece of his mind. He said Angelo was very strict and would call people out in public in the most embarrassing ways. He confronted strangers for smoking and other non-Christian acts likely as a result of his Methodism.

[98] Primary source: Frank's son, Richard Owen Bartholomew 2017

Mae got pregnant out of wedlock. By June of 1915 she is no longer in the picture. She was kicked out of the house, likely, and sometime that year, her son, Paul, was born. She had given Paul, Lena's new last name when she married Leon Gerowe.

Frank said he ran away from home when he was 14. We know he was still in Geddes in June, per the New York census and would have been 14 until October 18.[99]

On the 1920 census, Frank is 19 and living with his mother. It is not known if he assumed his step dad's last name but the census has him listed as Frank Gerowe. He was working with his step dad who was a mechanic and Frank is listed as an apprentice but both the same kind of work. The work line is unintelligible but whatever it is it is clear they are the same. The 1920 census he resided in Yonkers. Later on in life he maintained Bartholomew as a surname so it Gerowe could have been an error by the census taker.

When Frank was 21 he married a woman in her forties. The marriage was short lived. There are no known offspring from this marriage. Shortly after, Frank married somebody more his age but that did not last long either. He had a live in girlfriend after that who might have reached common law marriage status at some point. That relationship ended and then came the matriarch for future generations, Edith Raphael. She was 22 years younger than he and they married sometime after 1945.

There are stories of Frank and Edith going to motorcycle rallies all around New York campaigning for Dwight Eisenhower for President. Edith was pregnant for many of those rallies with Richard Bartholomew though some say she was pregnant with David Bartholomew. Richard was born in June of 1952 and David after so it is more likely that she was pregnant with

---

[99] Ibid. Richard Owen Bartholomew

Richard.

Most of the jobs that Frank had were driving jobs in New York City. Legend has it that he was driving a cab and the passenger tried to ditch on his fare. Frank chased the guy down, grabbed the guy's shirt under his collar. He pushed the guy away with still grasping his shirt, pulled him back and knocked the guy out. The legend continues with the guy he knocked out was a professional boxer.

He drove delivery trucks in Manhattan, as well at from time to time had one of his children ride with him. With his children, they lived in Far Rockaway's and Center Moriches so he always commuted to a driving job. When it came to trips anywhere even within Queens, Frank did not drive and would make excuses not to drive.

One time they loaded the children in the car to take them to see Mae and her family who lived in Upstate New York just north of the city. At the toll Frank asked how much further ahead to their destination. They got to their destination town but in Connecticut instead of New York. What should have been a short trip turned into an all day adventure.

In 1960 Edith had enough and moved out of the house. One of their final arguments, he said something along the lines of, "I hope you die," to which she replied, "I'll live longer than you". He died at the age of 67 in 1968 and she died at the age of 69 in 1992 and beat him by a few months.

From that point on he raised Mark, Richard, David and Neil near a duck farm in Center Moriches. Patricia may have lived with them too but she was near being of age.

Frank was a small time collector of junk after 1960. He always traded vehicles away and got newer vehicles to him though usually model years behind the vehicle he traded away. With his background as a mechanic he tinkered on vehicles all the time, which probably helped as a professional driver if he could work on his own cars too

Frank died of emphysema in June of 1968. As strong of as man as he became with the left side of his body, throughout the sixties his stamina finally wore down. He died laying on the couch with his hands over his chest like he'd done many times for a nap. The irony is Angelo petitioned against smoking and other things, which would, do harm to the body from a religious perspective. The irony was the smoking Angelo was against and what Frank rebelled and did, is what killed him.

The family branch goes back to 1425 and it appears every male in direct line to Frank, had faith in Jesus. Frank not only rejected his father's concerns about smoking, but also his religion. There have been secondary witnesses who have said Frank changed his views on his deathbed. One person said even in a dream they had received some knowledge of Frank's salvation. There is not any firm confirmation of this but these are the things that have been reported. But in God's graciousness it is possible.

Edith Raphael August 28,1922 – April 4, 1992

Edith receives her own chapter because to the contemporaries of this study, she is the most known. To some she was known as mom, to others she was known as Nana. One of her favorite phrases to her grandchildren was, "Kisses are so delicious."

She was born to Benjamin 1898-1934 and Jeanette Enzel 1899-1971. Raphael was pronounced often times as Raphale so much so that some public records show it spelled as it sounds.

Edith's entire ancestry can be traced to the Kingdom of Poland and is entirely Jewish. Depending on the time that a public record is taken, Russia is used as the country of origin because Poland would not have been a legitimate country of origin to use.

Many of the families came over during the late 1880's to 1890's. The hostility towards Jews in Poland was high. In 1881, for example, on Christmas Day, there was a false alarm about a fire at Holy Cross Church in Warsaw, Poland. The rumors were that they were pickpockets and that those pickpockets were Jewish boys. This escalated persecution against Jews in Warsaw and a mass exodus due to pogrom started. There have been many of these pogroms over the years from all around the world but this specifically happened in Warsaw following the false alarm. It turned out to be unsubstantiated but pogroms continued to escalate throughout Poland and floods of Jews fled the persecution and genocide. Edith's ancestors all left prior to World War II but most prior to World War I.

Edith had become pregnant prior to be married. She got kicked out of the house. She sought and found refuge with The Salvation Army in New York City though which borough is not known. She had Bruce in 1939 or 1940 and he lived to be 22 months old likely from Pneumonia. Per the April 12, 1940 census Bruce was not listed. It's likely he hadn't been born yet. Her father, Benjamin Raphael died in 1934 so he wouldn't have been the one to kick her out of the house. Her Uncle, William Enzel was a resident of the same household in 1940 with Jeanette Raphael (Enzel) as head of household. It's said that her mother Jeannette likely would have been the one who kicked Edith out of the home. Jeanette had a mean streak

She lost her father, her baby and her home in an 8-year span. However, during that 8 year span, while she was at the Salvation Army, she converted to Christianity through the organization and maintained the Christian faith to her deathbed and when she could not maintain her Christian faith, her savior maintained it for her.

Before Edith met Frank, she had Patricia in 1945. The family never talked about Patricia being from another father than Frank. It was always assumed when they were growing up but the math was done and the years did not match up from when she met Frank and when Patricia was born. It wasn't until Edith's death that Patricia came clean about it and found out everyone else already knew.

Frank was 22 years her senior and their first child together was Mark who was born in 1950. Their second son was Richard, born in 1952, David was born in 1954 and Neil was born in 1956.

The term deathbed for Edith was different than for anyone else as she was sick for half of her life. When she was around 35 years of age she had been diagnosed with leukemia, which attacks white blood cells, and she was also known to have had a rare Jewish ethnic disease that attacked her red blood cells. She was diabetic and also had lupus as well as other complications.

Edith and Frank had a lot of tension after Neil was born. There were many fights and finally Edith had enough and moved out in 1960, leaving her children behind. Frank moved them out to Center Moriches at that time and there was a lot of resentment from the children towards their mother.

Frank died in 1968 and Richard, David and Neil had to move in with Edith on Long Beach.

Richard stated he resented the move and spent as much time with Patricia as possible. Mark enlisted in the Air Force during the height of the Vietnam War and stationed in Thailand.

Edith attended St. John's By the Sea Lutheran Church. She forced Richard to go through adult confirmation and she attended with him. Richard went reluctantly but became a Christian as a result and went on to become a Lutheran Pastor.

David became a real estate agent until he got hired on to the NYPD and earned his gold shield within 5 years.

Neil developed some disabilities from unknown causes and also was diagnosed with schizophrenia. He however was able to work for Nassau County sewage treatment as a facility janitor and received state pension as a result.

Edith moved closer to Albany as she got older and died there in 1992. She is buried at Holy Cross Lutheran Cemetery in Glenmont, NY.

The 1940 census has Edith listed as a retail sales lady in millinery. The line above, occupied by Jeanette was left blank but Jeanette worked in retail sales at the high end B Altman and Co. store. Richard remembers for Christmas they would get gifts from B Altman every year.

Edith's parents were Benjamin Raphael (1898-1934) and Jeanette Enzel (1899-1971). Benjamin's parents were Abraham Raphael (1870-1954) and Rebecca Kantrowitz (1875-1947). They were the first to migrate to the United States. On the Raphael side, there is no history prior to those who had not migrated. The same is true not true on the Enzel side but what is known about the prior generation is limited to names. Jeanette was the daughter of Jacob Enzel (1862-1913) and Tillie Hoffman (1863-1935). Jacob was son of Isidore Enzel and Jennie Cohn both birth dates and deaths unknown. Tillie was the daughter of Michael Hoffman and Frances Green

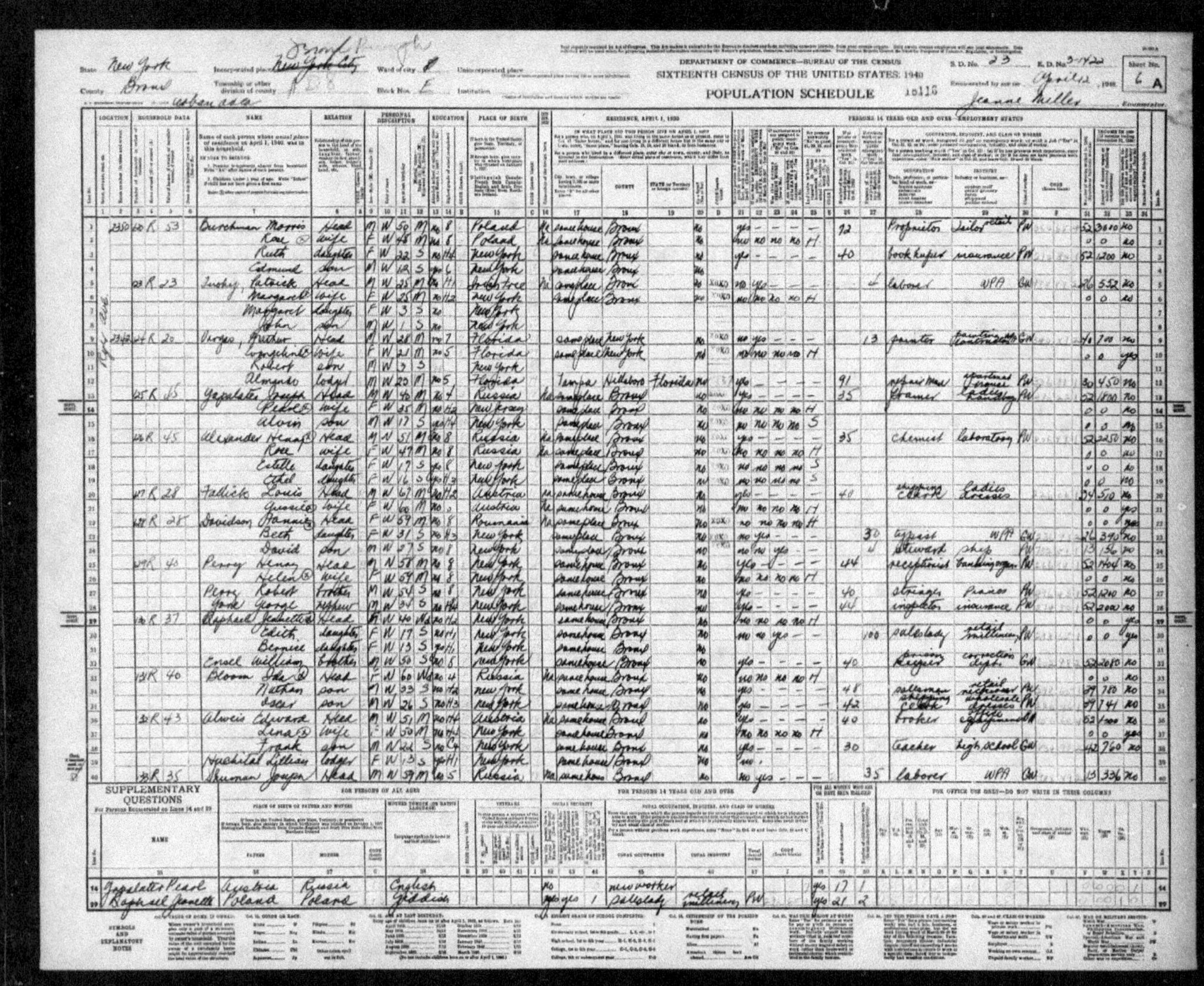

State: New York | Incorporated place: ~~New York City~~ Bronx Borough | Ward of city: 8 | Block No.: E | County: Bronx | Township or other division of county: [illegible] | S. D. No. 23 | E. D. No. 3-1422 | Sheet No. 6 A

DEPARTMENT OF COMMERCE—BUREAU OF THE CENSUS

SIXTEENTH CENSUS OF THE UNITED STATES: 1940

POPULATION SCHEDULE 18118

Enumerated by me on April 12, 1940. Jeanne Miller, Enumerator

Line	House no.	Household no.	Home owned or rented	Value or rent	Name	Relation	Sex	Race	Age	Marital	School	Grade	Place of birth	Citizenship	Residence 1935: city	County	State	Farm	Col. 21	Col. 22	Col. 23	Col. 24	Col. 25	Hours (26)	Weeks unemployed (27)	Occupation	Industry	Class	Weeks worked (31)	Income (32)	Other income (33)
1	2350	60	R	53	Burchman, Morris	Head	M	W	50	M	no	8	Poland	Na	same house	Bronx		no	yes	–	–	–	–	72		Proprietor	tailor retail	PW	52	3010	no
2					Rose ⊗	wife	F	W	48	M	no	8	Poland	Na	same house	Bronx		no	no	no	no	no	H						0	0	no
3					Ruth	daughter	F	W	22	S	no	H4	New York		same house	Bronx		no	yes	–	–	–	–	40		bookkeeper	insurance	PW	52	1200	no
4					Edmund	son	M	W	12	S	yes	6	New York		same house	Bronx		no													
5		23	R	23	Twohy, Patrick	Head	M	W	25	M	no	H1	Irish Free State	Na	same place	Bronx		no	no	yes	–	–	–		4	laborer	WPA	GW	26	552	no
6					Margaret ⊗	wife	F	W	25	M	no	H2	New York		same place	Bronx		no	no	no	no	no	H						0	0	no
7					Margaret	daughter	F	W	3	S	no		New York																		
8					John	son	M	W	1	S	no		New York																		
9	2342	24	R	20	Vargas, Arthur	Head	M	W	28	M	no	7	Florida		same place	New York		no	no	yes	–	–	–		13	painter	painting contractor	GW	40	700	no
10					Evangeline ⊗	wife	F	W	21	M	no	5	Florida		same place	New York		no	no	no	no	no	H						0	0	yes
11					Robert	son	M	W	3	S			New York																		
12					Almando	lodger	M	W	20	M	no	5	Florida		Tampa	Hillsboro	Florida	no	yes	–	–	–	–	91		repair man	apartment houses	PW	30	450	no
13		25	R	35	Yapalater, Joseph	Head	M	W	40	M	no	4	Russia	Na	same place	Bronx		no	yes	–	–	–	–	35		framer	ladies handbag	PW	52	1800	no
14					Pearl ⊗	wife	F	W	35	M	no	H2	New Jersey		same place	Bronx		no	no	no	no	no	H						0	0	no
15					Alvin	son	M	W	17	S	yes	H4	New York		same place	Bronx		no	no	no	no	no	S						0	0	no
16		26	R	45	Alexander, Henry ⊗	Head	M	W	51	M	no	8	Russia	Na	same place	Bronx		no	yes	–	–	–	–	35		chemist	laboratory	PW	52	2250	no
17					Rose	wife	F	W	47	M	no	8	Russia	Na	same place	Bronx		no	no	no	no	no	H						0	0	no
18					Estelle	daughter	F	W	17	S	yes	8	New York		same place	Bronx		no	no	no	no	no	S						0	0	no
19					Ethel	daughter	F	W	16	S	yes	H3	New York		same place	Bronx		no	no	no	no	no	S						0	0	no
20		27	R	28	Fallick, Louis	Head	M	W	67	M	no	H2	Austria	Na	same house	Bronx		no	yes	–	–	–	–	40		shipping clerk	ladies dresses		34	510	no
21					Jessie ⊗	wife	F	W	60	M	no	0	Austria	Na	same house	Bronx		no	no	no	no	no	H						0	0	yes
22		28	R	28	Davidson, Fannie ⊗	Head	F	W	59	M	no	8	Roumania	Na	same place	Bronx		no	no	no	no	no	H						0	0	yes
23					Beth	daughter	F	W	31	S	no	H3	New York		same place	Bronx		no	no	yes	–	–	–		30	typist	WPA	GW	26	390	no
24					David	son	M	W	27	S	no	8	New York		same place	Bronx		no	no	no	yes	–	–		4	steward	ship	PW	13	156	no
25		29	R	40	Perry, Henry	Head	M	W	58	M	no	8	New York		same house	Bronx		no	yes	–	–	–	–	44		receptionist	banking organ.	PW	52	1404	no
26					Helen ⊗	wife	F	W	59	M	no	8	New York		same house	Bronx		no	no	no	no	no	H						0	0	no
27					Perry, Robert	brother	M	W	54	S	no	8	New York		same house	Bronx		no	yes	–	–	–	–	40		stringer	pianos	PW	52	1210	no
28					York, George	nephew	M	W	34	S	no	H4	New York		same house	Bronx		no	yes	–	–	–	–	44		inspector	insurance	PW	52	2000	no
29		30	R	37	Raphael, Jeanette ⊗	Head	F	W	40	Wd	no	H2	New York		same house	Bronx		no	no	no	no	no	H						0	0	yes
30					Edith	daughter	F	W	17	S	no	H1	New York		same house	Bronx		no	no	no	yes	–	–		100	saleslady	retail millinery	PW	0	0	yes
31					Bernice	daughter	F	W	13	S	yes	H1	New York		same house	Bronx		no													
32					Ensel, William	brother	M	W	50	S	no	8	New York		same house	Bronx		no	yes	–	–	–	–	40		prison keeper	correction dept.	GW	52	2080	no
33		31	R	40	Bloom, Ida ⊗	Head	F	W	60	Wd	no	4	Russia	Na	same house	Bronx		no	no	no	no	no	H						0	0	no
34					Nathan	son	M	W	33	S	no	H2	New York		same house	Bronx		no	yes	–	–	–	–	48		salesman	retail neckwear	PW	39	780	no
35					Oscar	son	M	W	26	S	no	H3	New York		same house	Bronx		no	yes	–	–	–	–	42		shipping clerk	wholesale dresses	PW	39	741	no
36		32	R	43	Alweis, Edward	Head	M	W	51	M	no	H4	Austria	Na	same house	Bronx		no	yes	–	–	–	–	40		broker	office equipment	OA	52	1400	no
37					Lena ⊗	wife	F	W	50	M	no	H4	New York		same house	Bronx		no	no	no	no	no	H						0	0	yes
38					Frank	son	M	W	22	S	no	C4	New York		same house	Bronx		no	yes	–	–	–	–	30		teacher	high school	GW	42	760	no
39					Hochital, Lillian	lodger	F	W	13	S	yes	H1	New York		same house	Bronx		no	no												
40		33	R	35	Shuman, Joseph	Head	M	W	59	M	no	5	Russia	Na	same house	Bronx		no	no	yes	–	–	–		35	laborer	WPA	GW	13	336	no

SUPPLEMENTARY QUESTIONS

For Persons Enumerated on Lines 14 and 29

Line	Name	Birthplace of father	Birthplace of mother	Mother tongue	Col. 42	Col. 43	Col. 44	Usual occupation	Usual industry	Class	Col. 48	Age at first marriage	Number of children
14	Yapalater, Pearl	Austria	Russia	English	no			new worker			yes	17	1
29	Raphael, Jeanette	Poland	Poland	Yiddish	yes	yes	1	saleslady	retail millinery	PW	yes	21	2

Roll and Muster of the Third Company fifth Conn^t Reg^t of Foot commanded by Lt Col^o Com^t Sherman for May 1782

Ranks.	Names.	Term of Inliftment.	Cafualties.	Muftered.	Time fince laft muftered, or inlifted.	Alterations fince laft Mufter.
Capt	Nehemiah Rice			Nehemiah Rice	May 22d 82	
Lieut	Joshua Whitney		On Com^d Lines June 7th 82		May 82	
Serj^t	Israel Cone	D. W.		Israel Cone	May 82	
	Ebenezer Hinkley	d°		Ebenezer Hinkley	May 82	
	David Dixon	d°	Recruit^g Com^d June		May 82	
	Thomas Spencer	d°		Thomas Spencer	May 82	
Corp^l	Amos Clark	d°		Amos Clark	May 82	
	John Daboll	d°		John Daboll	April 25th 82	
	Samuel Jackson	d°		Samuel Jackson	May 82	
Drum	Elijah Pixlee	d°		Elijah Pixlee	May 82	
Fife	David Phelps	d°		David Phelps	April 82	
Privates 1	David Brown	4 Y 1 C		David Brown	April 82	
2	Samuel C. Heath	D. W.		Samuel C. Heath		Join^d from Des^t May 26
3	Jesse Matthews	d°		Jesse Matthews	May 82	
4	Timothy Stedman			Timothy Stedman		Join^d from Detachm^t May 9th
5	Eli Denslow			Eli Denslow	May 82	
6	Simeon Taylor			Simeon Taylor	May 82	
7	Ithamar Olney	20 Days		Ithamar Olney	May 82	
8	Jonathan Gaylord	14 6M		Jonathan Gaylord	May 82	
9	Palamon Abernathy			Palamon Abernathy	March 1st 82	Join^d May 29th 82
10	George Fields	D. W.		George Fields	May 82	
11	Elkel Scott			Elkel Scott	May 82	
12	Samuel Mitchel			Samuel Mitchel	May 82	
13	Cornelius Phelps	9 Months		Cornelius Phelps	March 25th 82	Join^d May 11th 82
14	Amos Westland	5 d°		Amos Westland	April 1st 82	Join^d May 30th 82
15	Prince Hotchkiss	D. W.		Prince Hotchkiss	April 25th 82	
16	Edward Jeremy	1 Month		Edward Jeremy	May 82	
17	Samuel Bartholomew	14. 6 M		Samuel Bartholomew	May 82	
18	David Smith	2 9		David Smith	April 17th 82	Join^d May 9th 82
19	Ezra Harvey	D. W.		Ezra Harvey	May 82	
20	John Cadwell	9 Months		John Cadwell	March 25th 82	Join^d May 9th 82
21	Reuben Martin	6 d°		Reuben Martin	May 82	
22	Zachariah Rolo	D. W.		Zachariah Rolo	May 82	
23	Reuben Sherman	14. 7 M		Reuben Sherman	May 82	
24	Roswell Hotchkiss	1 6		Roswell Hotchkiss	May 82	
25	Stephen Read	1 6		Stephen Read	May 82	
26	Benjamin Bingham	D. W.		Benjamin Bingham	May 82	
27	George W. Shipman	14. 7 M		George W. Shipman	April 25th 82	
28	John Lines	1 9		John Lines	May 82	
29	Ezra Sibley	1 6		Ezra Sibley	May 82	
30	Levi Hitchcock	D. W.	Northfield Waggoner Dec 1 81		June 1st 81	
31	John Marsh	D. W.	Sick Northampton Aug 3d 81		Aug 3d 81	
	Daniel Cone	14. 6 M			May 82	Transferd Invalids June 1st 82
	Abdiel Flowers	D. W.			May 82	
	Isaiah Moss	d°			May 82	

I Certify the above Roll to be the true State of faid Comp^y this fourteenth Day of June 1782

N. Rice Capt

I Certify the above Mufter to be true in all its Contents.

Infpection of May 1782

Steuben Maj^r Genl

Infpector General of the Army of the United States

Roll and Muster of the 3d Company 5th Conn.t Regiment of Foot commanded by Lieut. Col. Comd.t Sherman for July 1782

Ranks.	Names.	Term of Inlistment	Casualties.	Mustered.	Time since last Mustered, or Inlisted.	Alterations since last Muster.
Captain	Nehemiah Rice			Nehemiah Rice	29th July 1782 for June	
Lieut.	Joshua Whitney			Joshua Whitney	do	
Sergeants	Isreal Cone	During War		Isreal Cone	29 July 1782 for June	
	Ebenezer Hinkley	do		Ebenezer Hinkley	do	
	David Dixon	do		David Dixon	do	
	Thomas Spencer	do		Thomas Spencer	do	
Corporals	Amos Clark	do		Amos Clark	do	
	John Daball	do		John Daball	do	
	Samuel Jackson	do		Samuel Jackson	do	
Drum	Elijah Riley	do		Elijah Riley	do	
Fife	David Phelps	do		David Phelps	do	
Privates	Jesse Matthews	do		Jesse Matthews	do	
2	Samuel C. Heath	do		Samuel C. Heath	do	
3	Eli Denslow	do		Eli Denslow	do	
4	Timothy Stedman	do		Timothy Stedman	do	
5	Levi Hitchcock	do		Levi Hitchcock	do	
6	Simeon Taylor	do		Simeon Taylor	do	
7	Ethel Scott	do		Ethel Scott	do	
8	George Fields	do		George Field	do	
9	Samuel Mitchel	do		Samuel Mitchel	do	
10	Benjamin Bingham	do		Benjamin Bingham	do	
11	Ezra Harvey	do		Ezra Harvey	do	
12	Prince Hotchkiss	do		Prince Hotchkiss	do	
13	John Marsh	do			March 1782	
14	Zachaniah Rolo	do		Zachaniah Rolle	... 9th 1782	
15	David Brown	Years 2		David Brown	do	
16	Palamon Abernathy	6		Palamon Abernathy	do	
17	Jonathan Gaylord	1 3		Jonathan Gaylord	do	
18	Cornelius Phelps	7		Cornelius Phelps	do	
19	Amos Westland	3		Amos Westland	do	
20	Samuel Bartholomew	1 4		Samuel Bartholomew	do	
21	David Smith	2 7		David Smith	do	
22	Reuben Martin	4		Reuben Martin	do	
23	John Cadwell	7		John Cadwell	do	
24	Reuben Sherman	1 5		Reuben Sherman	do	
25	Roswell Hotchkiss	1 4		Roswell Hotchkiss	do	
26	Stephen Reed	1 3		Stephen Reed	do	
27	George Wm. Shipman	1 5		George Wm. Shipman	do	
28	Ezra Sibley	1 4		Ezra Sibley	do	
29	John Lines	1 7		John Lines	do	
30	Elijah Kibbee	4		Elijah Kibbe	do	
31	Ephraim Webster	4		Ephraim Webster	July 9th 1782	Joined July 24 82
32	John Dowing	4		John Downing	June 5th 82	17
33	James Patchen	4		James Patchen	April 26 82	July 24
34	William Reed	4		Stephen Reed	June 10th 82	17
35	Jason Hitchcock					
36	Edward Holmes					

I Certify the above Roll to be the true State of said Company this twentyninth Day of July 1782

Nehemiah Rice Capt

I Certify the above Muster to be true in all its Contents.

Inspection of July 1782

J. Barber Major

Dpt. Inspector of the north Army.

Chapter

Roll and Muster of the 3d Company 5th Connecticut Regt. of Foot Commanded by Lt. Col. Comdt. Sherman for Octr.

Ranks.	Names.	Term of Inlistment.	Casualties.	Mustered.	Time since last Muster, or Inlistment.	Alterations since last Muster.
Capt.	Nehemiah Rice			Nehemiah Rice	Octr. 1st 1782	
Lieut.	Joshua Whitney			Joshua Whitney	do	
Serjts.	Israel Cone	3 war		Cone	Octr. 1 1782	
	Ebenr. Hinkley	8	Furlough by Genl. Huntington [illegible]		August 82	
	David Dixon	8		Dixon	Octr.	
	Thomas Spencer	8		Spencer	do	
Corpls.	Amos Clark	8		Clark	do	
	John Dabolt	8		Dabolt	do	
	Samuel Jackson	8	On Duty Genl. McDougals		do	
Drum	Elijah Pixly	8		Pixly	do	
	David Phelps	8		Phelps	do	
Privates No. 1	John Matthews	8		Matthews	do	
2	Samuel Heath	8	On Comnd. 30 Octr. 82		do	
3	Timothy Stedman	8		Stedman	do	
4	Levi Hitchcock	8	On Comnd. [illegible]		do	
5	Simeon Taylor	8		Taylor	do	
6	Eli Denslow	8	Sick N. Windsor Sept. 1st 82		Sept. 82	
7	Ethel Scott	8		Scott	Octr.	
8	Samuel Mitchel	8		Mitchel	do	
9	Benjamin Bingham	8		Bingham	do	
10	Ezra Harvey	8		Harvey	do	
11	Prince Hotchkiss	8		Prince Hotchkiss	do	
12	John Marsh	8	Sick [illegible] August [illegible] 81		Sept. 82	
13	Zachariah Rolls	8		Rolls	Octr. 82	
		months. days				
14	David Brown	12 20		Brown	do	
15	Jonathan Gaylord	10 6	On duty		Sept. 82	
16	Samuel Bartholomew	14 . 6		Bartholomew	Octr. 82	
17	David Smith	29 . 5		Smith	do	
18	Reuben Sherman	14 . 20		Sherman	do	
19	Asahel Hotchkiss	14 . 2		Hotchkiss	do	
20	Ezra Sibley	13 . 20		Sibley	do	
21	Elisha Parrish	29 . 12		Parrish	do	
22	Stephen Rice	12 29		Rice	do	
23	John Lines	16 18		Lines	Sept. 82	
24	John Cadwell	4 . [illegible]	On Comnd. [illegible]		Octr.	
25	John Downing	6 20	Sick New Boston 20th Sept. 82		Sept.	
26	Solomon Abernethy	3 . 20	On Comnd. [illegible]		do	
27	Cornelius Phelps	4 . 15	do		do	
28	Ephraim Webster	1 . 20	do		do	
29	Edward Holmes	5 . 2	do		do	
30	Amos Westland	— 20	do		do	
31	Reuben Martin	1 . 20	do		do	
32	Elijah Kibbee	1 . 20	do		do	
33	James Polchon	1 20	do		do	
34	William Reed	1 . 20	do		do	
35	Jason Hitchcock	1 20	do		do	

I Certify the above Roll to be the true State of said Compy this 20th Day of Octr 1782

Nehemiah Rice Captn

I Certify the above Muster to be true in all its Contents.

Inspection of [illegible] 1782

[illegible] Major & Asst. Inspector of [illegible] Army.

Ancillary Data

Roll and Muster of *the 3 Comp^y in the 5th Connecticut Regiment of foot commanded by Lt Col. Sherman*

Ranks.	Names.	Term of Inliftment.	Cafualties.	Muftered.	Time fince laft muftered, or inlifted.	Alterations fince laft Mufter.
Capt	Nehemiah Rice			Nehemiah Rice	Augt 3 81	
Lt	Joshua Whitney			Joshua Whitney	March 1st 82	
Sergt	Israel Cone	D. War		Israel Cone	March 1st 1782	
	Ebenezer Hinkley	D. War		Ebenezer Hinkley	July 9th 81	
	David Dixson	D. War		David Dixson	March 1st 82	
	Thomas Spencer	D. War		Thomas Spencer	Feby 1 82	
Corpls	Amos Clark	D. War	On Duty Lines Apl 12th 82	Amos Clark	March 1 82	
	John Daboll	D. War		John Daboll	March 1 82	
Drum	Elijah Bixlee	D. War		Elijah Bixlee	Feby 1st 82	
	Gideon Moody	1 y 8 m	[illegible]		Feby 1 82	Transferd to Lt Co. Apl 26th 1782
Fife	David Phelps	D. War	[illegible]	David Phelps	March 1st 82	
Privates 1	Samuel Bartholomew	1 year 8 month		Samuel Bartholomew	March 1 82	
2	David Brown	1 8		David Brown	March 1 82	
3	Daniel Cone	7		Daniel Cone	Feby 1st 82	
4	Eli Denslow	During War		Eli Denslow	March 1st 82	
5	Ozias Elwell	D. War		Ozias Elwell	Novr 2d 80	
6	George Fields	D. War		George Fields	Jany 1st 82	
7	Jonathan Gaylord	1 y 7 m	On Duty at Lines Apl 12th 82	Jonathan Gaylord	March 1st 82	
8	Ezra Harvey	D. War		Ezra Harvey		Joined March 82
9	Levi Hitchcock	D. War	Waggoner Conn Novr 1st 82		June 1st 81	
10	Roswell Hotchkiss	1 y 8 m		Roswell Hotchkiss	March 1st 82	
11	Prince Hotchkiss	D. War		Prince Hotchkiss	March 1 82	
12	Edward Jeremy	1 y 3 m		Edward Jeremy	March 1 82	
13	John Loines	1 11		John Loines	March 1 82	
14	John Marsh	D. War	Sick New Windsor Augt 8th 82	[illegible]	Augt 3d 81	
15	Jesse Matthews	D. War		Jesse Matthews	March 1st 82	
16	Samuel Mitchel	D. War		Samuel Mitchel	March 1st 82	
17	Isaiah Moss	D. War		Isaiah Moss	March 1 82	
18	Thomas Olney	1 y 2 m		Thomas Olney	March 1 82	
19	James Prout	1 9		James Prout	March 1st 82	
20	Zachariah Rolo	D. War		Zachariah Rolo	March 1 82	
21	Stephen Reed	1 y 7 m	On Duty at Lines Apl 12th 82	Stephen Reed	March 1st 82	
22	Ethel Scott	D. War	On Duty at Lines Feby 12th 82	Ethel Scott	Augt 3d 81	
23	George W. Shipman	1 y 9 m		George W. Shipman	Feby 1 82	
24	Reuben Sherman	1 9		Reuben Sherman	March 1 82	
25	Ezra Sibley	1 8		Ezra Sibley	Feby 1 82	
26	Simeon Taylor	D. War		Simeon Taylor	March 1 82	
27	Reuben Martin	y m		Reuben Martin	Jany 1st 82	joined April 6th 82

I Certify the above Roll to be the true State of said *Company* this *twenty fifth* Day of *April* 1782 —
Nehemiah Rice Capt

I Certify the above Muster to be true in all its Contents.
Inspection *For March* 1782
Steuben Maj. Genl.
Inspector *Genl.* of the Army *of the United States*

Roll and Muster of the 3d Company 5th Connt Regt of Foot commanded by Lt Col Comdt Sherman for August 1782

Ranks.	Names.	Term of Inlistment.	Casualties.	Mustered.	Time since last Muster, or Inlistment.	Alterations since last Muster.
Capt	Nehemiah Rice			Nehemiah Rice	Augt 1st 1782	
Lieut	Joshua Whitney			Joshua Whitney	do	
Sergt	Israel Cone	During War		Israel Cone	Augt 1st 82	
	Ebenr Hitchcock	do	Sick in Hospital Augt 27th 82		do	
	David Dixon	do		David Dixon	do	
	Thomas Spencer	do		Thomas Spencer	do	
Corpl	John Dabell	do		Amos Clark	do	
	Amos Clark	do		John Dabell	do	
	Samuel Jackson	do		Samuel Jackson	do	
Drumr	Elijah Pixlee	do		Elijah Pixlee	do	
Fife	David Phelps	do		David Phelps	do	
Privates 1	John Matthews	do		John Matthews	do	
2	Samuel Heath	do		Samuel Heath	do	
3	Eli Denslow	do	Sick in Camp	Eli Denslow	do	
4	Timothy Stedman	do		Timothy Stedman	do	
5	Levi Hitchcock	do		Levi Hitchcock	do	
6	Simeon Taylor	do		Simeon Taylor	do	
7	Ethel Stott	do		Ethel Stott	do	
	George Fields	do			do	
8	Samuel Mitchel	do		Samuel Mitchel	do	
9	Benjamin Bingham	do		Benjamin Bingham	do	
10	Ezra Harvey	do		Ezra Harvey	do	
11	Prince Hotchkiss	do		Prince Hotchkiss	do	
12	John Marsh	do		John Marsh	Jany 1st 1782	
13	Zachariah Rolo	do		Zachariah Rolo	Augt 1st 1782	
14	David Brown	Years Months 1 .. 3		David Brown	do	
15	Solomon Abernathy	.. 6		Solomon Abernathy	do	
16	Jonathan Gaylord	1 .. 2		Jonathan Gaylord	do	
17	Cornelius Phelps	.. 6		Cornelius Phelps	do	
18	Amos Westland	.. 2		Amos Westland	do	
19	Samuel Bartholomew	1 .. 3		Samuel Bartholomew	do	
20	David Smith	2 .. 6		David Smith	do	
21	Reuben Martin	.. [illegible]		Reuben Martin	do	
22	John Cadwell	.. 6		John Cadwell	do	
23	Reuben Sherman	1 .. 4		Reuben Sherman	do	
24	Roswell Hotchkiss	1 .. 3		Roswell Hotchkiss	do	
25	Stephen Read	1 .. 2		Stephen Read	do	
26	Ezra Sibley	1 .. 3		Ezra Sibley	do	
27	John Lines	1 .. 6		John Lines	do	
28	Elijah Kibbee	.. 3		Elijah Kibbee	do	
29	Ephraim Webster	.. 3		Ephraim Webster	do	
30	John Downing	.. 3		John Downing	do	
31	James Patchin	.. 3		James Patchin	do	
32	William Read	.. 3		William Read	do	
33	Jason Hitchcock	.. 3		Jason Hitchcock	April 17th 1782	Join'd Augt 1st 82
34	Edward Holmes	.. 7		Edward Holmes	... 13 82	July 29 82
35	Eliphaz Parrish	2 .. 7		Eliphaz Parrish	... 24 82	Augt 8 82
	George W. Shipman		transfd to Lt Infy Co			transfd to L Infy Co
	George Fields		do			do

I Certify the above Roll to be the true State of said Compy this ninth Day of September 1782

Nehh Rice Capt

I Certify the above Muster to be true in all its Contents. Inspection of August 1782

Walter Stewart Inspector of Northn Army.

Roll and Muster of the 3 Company 5th Connecticut Regiment of Foot commanded by Lieut Col Comd^t Sherman for April 1782

Ranks.	Names.	Term of Inlistment.	Casualties.	Mustered.	Time since last mustered, or inlisted.	Alterations since last Muster.
Captain	Nehemiah Rice			Nehemiah Rice	April 25th 1782	
Lieutenant	Joshua Whitney			Joshua Whitney	April .. 82	
Serj^ts	Israel Cone	Dur of War		Israel Cone	April 25th 82	
	Ebenezer Hinkley	do		Ebenezer Hinkley	April .. 82	
	David Dixon	do		David Dixon	April .. 82	
	Thomas Spencer	do		Thomas Spencer	April .. 82	
Corp^ls	Amos Clark	Dur of War		Amos Clark	April .. 82	
	John Dabell	do	On Duty at Lines May 16th 82	[illegible]	April .. 82	
	Samuel Jackson	do	Sick in Camp	Samuel Jackson	April .. 82	Join^d from 7th Comp^y May 1st 82
Drum	Elijah Bixlee	do		Elijah Bixlee	April .. 82	
Fife	David Phelps	do	On Duty at Lines May 16th 82	[illegible]	April .. 82	
Privates	1 Samuel Bartholomew	Years Months 1 7		Samuel Bartholomew	April .. 82	
	2 Benjamin Bingham	Dur of War		Benjamin Bingham	April 4th 82	Join^d April 26th 1782
	3 David Brown	y m 1 7	On Duty at Lines May 16th 82	[illegible]	April 25 .. 82	
	4 John Cadwell	.. 10		[illegible]	March 25 .. 82	Join^d May 9th 82
	5 Daniel Cone	1 6		Daniel Cone	April 25 .. 82	
	6 Eli Denslow	Dur of War		Eli Denslow	April 25 .. 82	
	7 George Fields	do		George Fields	April .. 82	
	8 Abdiel Flowers	do		Abdiel Flowers		Join^d from Desertion April 26th 82
	9 Jonathan Gaylord	y m 1 6	[illegible]	Jonathan Gaylord	April 25 82	
	10 Levi Hitchcock	Dur of War	Waggoner New Fairfield Oct 1st 82		June 1st 81	
	11 Ezra Harvey	do		Ezra Harvey	April 25 82	
	12 Roswell Hotchkiss	y m 1 7		Roswell Hotchkiss	April .. 82	
	13 Prince Hotchkiss	Dur of War	On Duty West point May 19th 82		April 82	
	14 Edward Jeremy	y m .. 2		Edward Jeremy	April 82	
	15 John Lines	1 10		John Lines	April 82	
	16 John Marsh	Dur of War	Sick New Windsor Aug 8th 82		Aug 3 81	
	17 Reuben Martin	y m .. 7		Reuben Martin	April 25 82	
	18 Jesse Matthews	Dur of War		Jesse Matthews	April 82	
	19 Samuel Mitchel	do		Samuel Mitchel	April .. 82	
	20 Isaiah Moss	do		Isaiah Moss	April .. 82	
	21 Ithamar Olney	y m .. 7		Ithamar Olney	April .. 82	
	22 Cornelius Phelps	.. 10		[illegible]	March 25 82	Join^d May 4th 82
	23 Stephen Read	1 .. 6		Stephen Read	April 25 82	
	24 Zachariah Rolo	Dur of War		Zachariah Rolo	April .. 82	
	25 Ethel Scott	do	Sick in Camp	Ethel Scott	April .. 82	
	26 Reuben Sherman	y m 1 8		Reuben Sherman	April .. 82	
	27 George W. Shipman	1 .. 8	On Duty at Lines May 16th 82	[illegible]	April .. 82	
	28 Ezra Sibley	1 7		Ezra Sibley	April 82	
	29 David Smith	2 10		[illegible]	April 17 82	Join^d May 9 82
	30 Timothy Stedman	Dur of War		[illegible]		Join^d from Desertion May 9th 82
	31 Simeon Taylor	do		Simeon Taylor	April 25 82	
	Ozias Elwell	do			April 82	Deserted April 26th 82
	James Brout	y m 1 8			April 82	Deserted April 26 82

I Certify the above Roll to be the true State of said Comp^y this twenty second Day of May - 1782

Nehemiah Rice Capt

I Certify the above Muster to be true in all its Contents. Inspection of April 1782

Walter Stewart Ass^t Inspector of North^n Army.

Roll and Muster of the third Company 5th Conn. Regiment of Foot commanded by Lieut Col. Comd. Sherman for June 1782

Ranks.	Names.	Term of Inlistment.	Casualties.	Mustered.	Time since last mustered, or inlisted.	Alterations since last Muster.
Captain	Nehemiah Rice			Nehemiah Rice	June 14th 82	
Lieut	Joshua Whitney			Joshua Whitney	May 22d 82	
Serjeants	Israel Cone	During War		Israel Cone	June 14th 82	
	Ebenezer Hinkley	do		Ebenezer Hinkley	14	
	David Dixon	do		David Dixon	May 22d 82	
	Thomas Spencer	do		Thomas Spencer	June 14 82	
Corpls	Amos Clark	do		Amos Clark	14	
	John Daball	do		John Dabold	14	
	Samuel Jackson	do		Samuel Jackson	14	
Drum	Elijah Pixlee	do		Elijah Pixlee	14	
Fife	David Phelps	do		David Phelps	14	
Privates No 1	Jesse Matthews	do		Jesse Matthews	14	
2	Samuel C. Heath	do		Samuel C. Heath	14	
3	Eli Denslow	do		Eli Denslow	14	
4	Timothy Stedman	do		Timothy Stedman	14	
5	Levi Hitchcock	do		Levi Hitchcock	June 1st 1782	
6	Simeon Taylor	do		Simeon Taylor	June 14	
7	Ethel Scott	do		Ethel Scott	14	
8	George Field	do		George Field	14	
9	Samuel Mitchel	do		Samuel Mitchel	14	
10	Benjamin Bingham	do		Benjamin Bingham	14	
11	Ezra Harvey	do		Ezra Harvey	14	
12	Prince Hotchkiss	do		Prince Hotchkiss	14	
13	John Marsh	do	Sick Northwinsor Aug 5th 81		Aug 5 1781	
14	Zachariah Rols	do		Zachariah Rols	June 14 82	
15	David Brown	Years [illegible] Months 5		David Brown	14	
16	Palamon Abernathy	7		Palamon Abernathy	14	
17	Jonathan Gaylord	1 4		Jonathan Gaylord	14	
18	Cornelius Phelps	8		Cornelius Phelps	14	
19	Amos Westland	4		Amos Westland	14	
20	Samuel Bartholomew	1 5		Samuel Bartholomew	14	
21	David Smith	2 8		David Smith	14	
22	Reuben Martin	6		Reuben Martin	14	
23	John Cadwell	8		John Cadwell	14	
24	Reuben Sherman	1 6		Reuben Sherman	14	
25	Roswell Hotchkiss	1 6		Roswell Hotchkiss	14	
26	Stephen Read	1 4		Stephen Read	14	
27	George Wm Shipman	1 6		George W. Shipman	14	
28	Ezra Sibley	1 5		Ezra Sibley	14	
29	John Lines	1 8		John Lines	14	
30	Elijah Kibbee	6		Elijah Kibbee	May 15th 82	Join'd June 15th 82
31	Ephraim Webster	6			July 9 82	Join'd July 24 82
32	John Downing	6			June 28 82	17
33	James Patchen	6			April 24 82	24
34	William Read	5			June 18 82	17
	Thomas Olney					Discharged July 1st 82
	Edward Jeremy					do July 25th 82

I Certify the above Roll to be the true State of said Company this 29th Day of July 1782

Nehh Rice Capt

I Certify the above Muster to be true in all its Contents. Inspection of June 1782

Walter Stewart Inspector of Northn Army.

Muster Roll of Captain Nehemiah Rice's Company 5th Connecticut Regiment in Service of the United States of America Commanded by Isaac Sherman Lieutenant Col. Commandant for May 1781

Commissioned { November 15th 1777 Captain Nehemiah Rice Furloughed May 21st 1781 for Fifteen Days
August 21st 1778 Lt. Joshua Whitney
January 1st 1778 Ensign Tiffany Command with the Light Infantry Feby 19th 1781

Appointed	Serjeants	Term	Remarks	Appointed	Corporals	Term	Remarks
	Israel Cone		Commissaries Clerk		Amos Clark		
	Ebenr Hinckley				Moses Culver		On Command L. Infantry Feby 1781
	Daniel Dixson				John Dabell		On Duty
	Thomas Spencer						
	Elijah Pike		Command L. Infantry Feby 19th 81				
	Drum				Fife		
	Elijah Pulie				David Phelps		
Inlisted	Privates			Inlisted	Privates		
	Samuel Bartholomew	During war			Pompey London		Sick in Quarters
	Jeremiah Booth	3 Years	Crampton on Duty		John Marsh		On Duty with Col. Drake
	David Brown	Ditto	Pines Bridge on Duty		Daniel Munrow		On Command L. Infantry Feby 19 81
	Bethel Camp	Ditto	Stoney Point Ditto		Samuel Mitchel		On Furlough in May 82
	Daniel Cone	Ditto	Kings Ferry Ditto		Jesse Matthews		Stoney Point on Duty
	Eli Denslow				Isaiah Moss		New Fairfield taken care of
	Caesar Doolittle	Ditto			John Mooney	3 Years	[illegible]
	Thomas Sapl		On Command L. Infantry Feby 19th		Zachariah Nole		Waggoner
Jany 19th 1781	Samuel Eldridge	3 Years	[illegible]		Stephen Price	Ditto	
	George Fields		[illegible]		Ethel Scott		
	James Griffens		[illegible]		George W. Shipman	Ditto	
Jany 24th 81	John Godfrey	Ditto	Joined May 1781	Jany 1st 1781	Reuben Sherman	3 Years	Joined May 10th 1781
	Levi Hitchcock			Ditto	Ezra Sibley	Ditto	Ditto Ditto
	Oswald Hotchkiss	Ditto		Jany 31st 1781	James Stoutt	Ditto	May 23 1781
	Prince Hotchkiss		Bennington on Duty		Simeon Tayler		
Jany 2 81	Nathaniel Johnston	3 Years	May the 23 1781		Humphrey Potter	Ditto	Deserted May 3 Ditto
					James Trout	Ditto	Ditto

June 1st 1781 Mustered then Capt. Rice's Company as Specified in the above Roll

D. Warner Sub Inspector 1st Brigade

Roll & Muster of the 2 Company Connecticutt Reg^t Commanded by Col^o Heman Swift. For the Month of July 1783

Rank	Names	Term of Inlistment	Casualties	Mustered	Time since last Muster	Alterations since last Muster
Capt.	Elias Stilwell	1 July 79		E. Stilwell	30 June 83	
Lieut.	Joshua Whitney	12 Aug. 80		J. Whitney	D°	
Serg^t	John Danielson	12 Months	Absent without leave		30th June 83	
—	Ezra Abby	5 D°		Abby	D°	
—	Abial Farnham	6 D°		Farnham	D°	
—	Fredrick Stores	10 D°		Stores	D°	
Corp^ls	Benjamin Tredwell	5 D°		Tredwell	30th June 83	
—	Elihu Dodge	5 D°		Dodge	D°	
—	Preserved Redway	6 D°		Redway	D°	
Fifer	Isaac Higgins	11 D°		Higgins	30th June 83	
Privates	Stephen Bennett	4 D°		Bennett	30th June 83	
2	Israel Clarke	4 D°		Clarke		
3	Sage Churchell	4 D°		Churchell		
4	David Butler	8 D°		Butler		
5	James Hall	10 D°		Hall		
6	Reuben Chapman	5 D°		Chapman		
7	George Harriss	6 D°		Harriss		
8	Luther Grover	7 D°		Grover		
9	Jehiel Wilcox	6 D°		Wilcox		
10	Amasa Grover	7 D°		Grover		
11	Clement Carr	5 D°		Carr		
12	Elijah Randol	4 D°		Randol		
13	John Whitman	5 D°		Whitman		
14	Israel Ransom	6 D°		Ransom		
15	Thos Bishop	4 D°		Bishop		
16	Moses Tracy	4 D°		Tracy		
17	Daniel Snyder	10 D°		Snyder		
18	Solomon Woodroff	4 D°		Woodroff		
19	Worth Armstrong	20 D°		Armstrong		
20	Timothy Woodbridge	4 D°	~~[illegible]~~	Woodbridge	14th March 83	
21	Asa Geer	8 D°		Geer	30 June 83	
22	Ebenezer Brown	10 D°		Brown		
23	Thos Manning	6 D°		Manning	—	
24	Thos Rathbone	6 D°		Rathbone		
25	Asa Sawyer	9 D°		Sawyer		
26	Saml Bartholomew	5 D°		Bartholomew		
27	Elimuth Elderkin	4 D°		Elderkin		
28	Stephen Bristor	5 D°		Bristor		
29	Jonathan Gaylor	4 D°		[illegible]		
30	Jessee Shepherd	4 D°		[illegible]		
31	Isaac Wardwell	5 D°		Wardwell		
32	Samuel Lane	5 D°		Lane		
33	Thos Densmore	22 D°		Densmore		
34	Nathaniel Clarke	6 D°		Clarke		
35	Simeon Cummins	6 D°		Cummins		
36	Jonathan Brown	5 D°		Brown		
37	Tim Sharper	8 D°		Sharper		
38	Ceasar Beamont	5 D°		Beamont		
39	Dick Bristor	5 D°		Bristor		
40	Juba Dyer	6 D°		Dyer		
41	Peter Bequiree	5 D°		Bequiree		
—	Stephen Barnum	—		—		Discharged 4 July 83. Time Expired
—	Permit Boisfy	20 D°		—		Deserted 10 July 83
—	Timothy Hotchkiss	4 D°		—		Discharged 13 July 83 Inability

I Certify the Above Roll to be the true State of the Company this 13th day of August 1783

E. Stilwell Capt.

I Certify the Above to be true in all its Contents
Inspection of July 1783

W. Barber, Major &
Ass^t Inspector of the northern Army

Roll and Muster of the 3d Company 5th Conn Regt of Foot commanded by Lieut Col Comdt Sherman for Septr 1782

Ranks.	Names.	Term of Inlistment.	Casualties.	Mustered.	Time since last Muster, or Inlistment.	Alterations since last Muster.
Capt	Nehemiah Rice			Nehemiah Rice	Septr 1st 1782	
Lt	Joshua Whitney			Joshua Whitney	do	
Sergt	Israel Cone	During War		Cone	Sept. 1st 1782	
	Eben Hinkley	do	Sick Mass Hosp Aug 27th 82		Aug 1st 1782	
	David Dixon	do		Dixon	Septr 1st 1782	
	Thomas Spencer	do		Spencer	do	
Corpl	Amos Clark	do		Clark	do	
	John Daboll	do		Daboll	do	
	Samuel Jackson	do		Jackson	do	
Drum	Elijah Riley	do		Riley	do	
Fife	David Phelps	do		Phelps	do	
Privates No 1	Jesse Matthews	do		Matthews	do	
2	Samuel Heath	do		Heath	do	
3	Eli Denslow	do	Sick New Windsor Sept 11th 82		do	
4	Timothy Stedman	do		Stedman	do	
5	Levi Hitchcock	do		Hitchcock	do	
6	Simeon Taylor	do		Taylor	do	
7	Ethel Scott	do		Scott	do	
8	Samuel Mitchel	do		Mitchel	do	
9	Benjamin Bingham	do		Bingham	do	
10	[illegible]	[illegible]		Hovey	do	
11	Prince Hotchkiss	do		Prince Hotchkiss	do	
12	John Marsh	do	Sick Flying Hospital Aug 5th 82	Marsh	do	
13	Zachariah Rolo	do		Rolo	do	
14	David Brown	Month Day 14..18		Brown	do	
15	Jonathan Gaylord	14..4	On duty Flying Hospital Sept 11th 82	Gaylord	do	
16	Saml Bartholomew	15..4		Bartholomew	do	
17	David Smith	30..3		Smith	do	
18	Reuben Sherman	15..18		Sherman	do	
19	Roswell Hotchkiss	15..0		Roswell Hotchkiss	do	
20	Ezra Sibley	14..18		Sibley	do	
21	Eliphaz Parrish	30..10		Parrish	do	
22	Stephen Read	13..27		Stephen Read	do	
23	John Lines	17..16		Lines	do	
24	John Cadwell	3..11	On Comd Aug 11th 82	~~Cadwell~~	do	
25	John Downing	2..18		Downing	do	
26	Solomon Abernathy	4..18	On Comd 2 M.G. Sept 26		do	
27	Cornelius Phelps	6..11	do		do	
28	Ephraim Webster	2..18	do		do	
29	Edward Holmes	5..30	do		do	
30	Amos Westland	1..18	On Comd Mass Hut Oct 5th		do	
31	Reuben Martin	2..18	do		do	
32	Elijah Kibbee	2..18	do		do	
33	James Patchen	2..18	do		do	
34	William Read	2..18	do		do	
35	Jason Hitchcock	2..18	do		do	

I Certify the above Roll to be the true State of said Company this thirteenth Day of Oct. 1782

Nehemiah Rice Capt

I Certify the above Muster to be true in all its Contents.

Inspection of [illegible] 1782

Inspector of [illegible] Army.

Muster Roll of Captain Nehemiah Rices Comp^y 6th Connecticut Regiment in Service of the United States of America Command^d by Lt Col^o J. Sherman for July 1781

179

Commissioned { Novr 16th 1777 Capt Nehemiah Rice
Augt 21st 1780 Lieu^t Joshua Whitney Tarry-town On Duty

Appoint^d	Serjeants	Term	Remarks
	Israel Cone	✓	Commissary's Clark
	Eben^r Hinkley	✓	
	David Dixson	✓	
	Thos Spencer	✓	On Command Fish Hill
	Drums		
	Elijah Pixlee	✓	
Jany 1st 81	Gideon Moody	3 years	
Inlisted	**Privates**		
July 22^d 81	Peletiah Alford	Decr 31st 81	
	Sam^el Bartholomew	3 years	On Comm^d West Point
	David Brown	✓ D^o	Confin^d
	James Brand	✓ D^o	
	Bethel Camp	✓ D^o	On Command Stoney Point
	Daniel Cone	✓ D^o	Confin^d
July 12th 81	Jared Cone	Decr 31st [illegible]	
[illegible] 81	Jonah Co[illegible]		[illegible]
July 7th 81	Samuel Dunt	31st Decr 81	
	Sam^el Eldrige	3 years	On Comm^d West Point
	George Fields	✓	
	James Griffen	✓	Philadelphia with Dr M. Gen
	John Godfree	✓ D^o	Block House Dobbs Ferry
	Willm Gibbs	✓ D^o	On Comm^d West Point
Decr 18th 80	Jon^th Gaylord	✓ D^o	
	Levi Hitchcock		Waggoner
	Roswell Hotchkiss	D^o	
July 5th 81	Benjn Hull	Decr 31st 81	
	Prince Hotchkiss		On Duty at Lines
	Nathl Johnson	3 years	On Comm^d Stoney Point

Appoint^d	Corporals	Term	Remarks
	Amos Clark	✓	
	John Daboll	✓	
	Fifes		
	David Phelps	✓	
	Simeon Guile	3 years	
Inlisted	**Privates**		
	Thomas Lewis	✓	North River Boating
	Pomp London	✓	On Comm^d West Point
	John Loines	3 years	D^o D^o
	John Marsh	✓	
	Saml Mitchel	✓	
	Jesse Matthews	✓	
	Isaiah Moss	✓	
July 6th 81	Thames Olney	[illegible]	
	[illegible]	✓	[illegible] Dobbs Ferry
	Stephen Reed	3 years	On Comm^d West Point
	Ethel Scott	✓	
July 3^d 81	Levi Scovill	Decr 31st 81	
	George Shipman	3 years	On Command Scouting
	Reuben Sherman	D^o	Command West Point
	Ezra Sibley	✓ D^o	
	James Shote	✓ D^o	
	Simeon Taylor	✓	Brigade B. Smith
July 5th 81	Ashbel Upson	Decr 31st 81	
June 30	Joseph Whittemore	1 year	
July 19th 81	Daniel Williams	Decr 31st 81	
	Simeon Guile	3 years	appoint^d Fifer July 24th 81

August 3^d 1781 Then Mustered Capt Rices Comp^y as specify^d in the above Roll
B. Warner L. Inspector

Muster Roll of Captain Nehemiah Rices Company 5th Connecticut Regiment in the Service of the United States of America Commanded by Isaac Sherman Lieutenant Col. Comdt. for June 1781

Commissioned { November 18th 1777 Captain Nehemiah Rice
August 25th 1780 Lieutenant Joshua Whitney
~~April~~ 22 1780 ~~Lieut.~~ Isaiah Tiffany Transferred to the Light Infantry June 1st 1781

Appointed	Serjeants	Term	Remarks
	Isreal Cone		Commissy Clerk
	Ebenezer Hinckley		
	David Dixson		
	Thomas Spencer		On command West Point
	Elijah Pike		Transferred Light Company July 1st 81
	Drummer		
	Elijah Pixlee		
Inlisted	Privates		
	Saml. Bartholomew	3 Years	On command West Point
	David Brown	Do	On Duty
Dec 13th 81	James Brand	Do	Do
	Bethel Camp	Do	On command Stoney Point
	Daniel Cone	Do	
	Eli Denslow		
	Saml. Eldridge	Do	On command West Point
	George Fields		On duty
	James Griffen		[illegible]
	John Gilfree	Do	On Duty
April 6th	William Gibbs	Do	On command West Point
Dec 13th 81	Simon Guile	Do	On duty
	Levi Hitchcock		Do
	Roswell Hotchkiss	Do	Do
	Prince Hotchkiss		Do
	Nathanl. Johnston	Do	Do
	Pomp Jordan		On command West Point

Appointed	Corporals	Term	Remarks
	Amos Clark		
	John Dabell		
	Moses Culver		Transferred Light Company July 1st 81
	Fife		
	David Phelps		On duty
Inlisted	Privates		
	Thomas Lewis		Returned from the Light Company June 1st 81 On duty
March 30th 81	John Lewis	3 Years	On command West Point
	John Marsh		On command Col. Durkee
	Saml. Mitchel		On duty
	Jesse Matthews		
	Isaiah Moss		
	Zachariah Pole		On duty
	Stephen Reed	Do	On command West Point
	Ethel Scott		
	George Sherman	Do	On duty
	Reuben Sherman	Do	On command West Point
	Ezra Sibley	Do	
	James Stout	Do	On duty
	Simeon Taylor		Blacksmith
	Thomas Card		Transferred Light Company July 1st 81
	Daniel Munnes		Do Do
	Caesar [illegible]	Do	Transferred [illegible] June 1st 81
	Jeremiah Booth	Do	Died July 6th 81
	John Mumey	Do	Deserted June 18th 81

July 9th 1781 Mustered then Captain Rices Company as Specified in the above Roll

David Smith Sub Inspector

Samuel Bartholomew enlisted as a private Soldier
in the year Seventeen hundred and seventy nine
in the Company Commanded by Captain Rice in the
fifth Connecticut Regiment Commanded by Col^o^
Sherman in the Connecticut Line - for three years
and served faithfully in the American Army
under the Continental Establishment untill
the Close of the aforesaid War - that he was disc-
-harged at West Point State of New York by General
Huntington with Honour - which discharge is worn out
and lost - the said Bartholomew further saith
... further evidence in his

State of New-York, } ss. Samuel Bartholomew being
OTSEGO COUNTY } duly sworn, saith, that he is a resident of the town of Unadilla in the County aforesaid, and has served as a private soldier in the war of the revolution against the common enemy, for the term of Nine Months and longer, at a certain period of the war herein after mentioned, on the Continental Establishment, and is yet a resident citizen of the United States; and by reason of his reduced circumstances in life, he is in need of assistance from his country for support. And this deponent further saith, that he never has received any pension from the United States, and doth hereby relinquish his claim to every pension that may have been heretofore allowed him by the laws of the United States, excepting and reserving to himself the right of claiming, and he doth hereby claim a pension under an act entitled "An act to provide for certain persons engaged in the land and naval service of the United States in the revolutionary war," passed 18th March, 1818. And this deponent doth further declare under oath, that the time he entered the army of the United States in the war of the revolution aforesaid, on the Continental Establishment, the officers under whom he served, and the line to which he belonged, together with the time and manner of leaving the service, are all correctly set forth, according to the best of his knowledge and recollection, in the following manner; that is to say, he the said —

6341

Albany, N. York

Elizabeth Bartholomew

widow of Saml. Bartholomew

who was a Private

in the Revolution

Inscribed on the Roll at the rate of
80 Dollars
Cents per annum, to commence on the 4th day of March, 1843.

Certificate of Pension issued the
5. day of Novr. 1844
and sent to A. H. Beach
Unadilla, N. York

[Act of March 3, 1843.]

Recorded in Book A.

13.301

New York

Samuel Bartholomew

of Unadilla in the state of New York
who was a Private &c in the regiment commanded by
Colonel [illegible] of the Connecticut

Unadilla Otsego County – N York
14th June 1821

Sir –

the public note of Mr J.L. Edwards I have received – to which I answer that there is a Man in the town of Unadilla by the name of Samuel Bartholomew – and is

now present who says that he first engage
in the Regiment Commanded by Col.o Sherman
and serv.d he thinks about two years when he
was Transfered to Col.o Huntingtons Reg.t
where he remained untill discharged at the
close of the war — that he never served in
Col.o Reeds Reg.t or any other than the two as
above mentioned —

Most respectfully
your Ob.d Serv.t
Abijah H. Beach

J. L. Edwards esquire
War Department

Unadilla Otsego County
State of New York 12th September 1843.

Dear Sir

I am earnestly Solicited to call your attention to the Pension application of the Widow Elizabeth Bartholomew of this place — her papers were Transmitted to the Pension Office the 24th of April 1842 — Your letter to me of 29th April 1842 states that she was not then allowed a pension because she was not a Widow at the time of passing the Act of 1838 her Husband having died in 1840 ...

Unadilla Otsego County
State of New York 5th March 1844

I return the enclosed Certificate supposing it was made by error or perhaps for some other person — and we give the following explanations — We claim pension for Elizabeth Bartholomew the Widow of Samuel Not Phillip Bartholomew — under the Act of 1838 for five years — Not 3d March 1843 — the said Samuel Bartholomew died 12th Decr 1840 — Not 16th Aug 1824 as may appear by her first and second application on file in the ...

if any new form or regulations is required - please send me a Copy

Most respectfully
Your Obt Servt
Elijah H. Beach

J. L. Edwards
Com. of Pensions

July 23d 44

War Department
Pension Office
Washington City

N.Y.
Mar 3d 1843

Unadilla Otsego County
State of New York 28th October 1844

Sir

I am so frequently call'd on for information as to the two following cases that I now write to enquire into the situation of them: viz Elizabeth Bartholomew the Widow of Samuel Bartholomew of this place who was pensioned under the Act of 1838 — and then on the 10th of July last sent a new application for the pension of of one year or continuation of pension under the Act of 3rd of March 1843 —

July 23
Decbr 43.

Also the case of Abigail Hull the Widow of David Hull of this place who made application for pension in November last 1843 which was return'd for want of more full evidence of Marriage — which was obtained and sent to Pension Office the 26th of August 1844 last — Nothing has been heard from those two Cases since — information is requested —

Most Respectfully
Your Obt Servt
Abijah H. Beach

Hon. James L. Edwards
Comsr of Pensions —

4087

the handwriting of said Justice and verily believe his Signature subscribed to the within Jurat and annexed certificate to be genuine

In Testimony whereof I have hereunto set my hand & official seal this 5th day of July A D 1841.

Geo. B. Wilson Clk

Treasury Department
3d Auditor's Office,
March 4, 1862.

Sir, I beg leave to refer the Enclosed Letter of Levi Bartholomew to your Office for a reply. Of which reference the writer has been informed.

Very Respectfully
[illegible]
Aud

Jos. H. Barrett Esq,
Com. of Pensions,

Waterford New London County
State of Connecticut
2nd March 1842

Sir

I sent you a line that there were no record of marriage of Elizabeth Butler but by making Enquery I find that there is three or four persons that does well remember about the wedding & one was at the wedding and stood up with the Bride & Groom that is Mrs Tillitson three of these will testify of the thing you want they are four or five miles from where I live but can be obtained you will Please to Direct

Yours in hast

E P Baker

State of New York
Otsego County ss } I Samuel Russell Clerk of said County do hereby certify that Charles C. Noble Esq. before whom the within affidavit of Rebecca Haynes purports to have been sworn was at the date of the same a Justice of the Peace in & for said County duly elected sworn and authorised to take the same and do further that I am well acquainted with the hand writing of said Justice and believe his name subscribed to same within affidavit certificate to be his genuine signature

Witness my hand and seal of office this 16th day of April 1842
Samuel Russell clk

Bartholomew of Unadilla — formerly Elizabeth Butler of Waterford in Connecticut — that she has always lived near her said Sister since they were Children — that she now well recollects her said Sister's Marriage with Samuel Bartholomew which took place at her Fathers House at Waterford - New London County State of Connecticut some time in the Month of January 1784 before Elder Darrow the Baptist Minister of that place — she cannot say on what day but thinks it was about the middle of January 1784 that she was at the Wedding

State of New-York, } ss. I [illegible] one of the
OTSEGO COUNTY, } Judges of the Court of Common Pleas in and for
the County aforesaid, do certify that I am satisfied the said Samuel Bartholomew
served in the revolutionary war as aforesaid, against the common
enemy, for a longer term than nine months, as stated in the affidavit of the said
Samuel Bartholomew hereunto annexed—And I do further certify
that full credit is due to the deposition of the above named John Haynes and
John Bartholomew and also that the evidence on which I have founded my
judgment is contained in the affidavit of the said Haynes & Bartholomew
and also my own personal knowledge of the said
Samuel Bartholomew and his [illegible]

[illegible] one
of the [illegible]

[illegible] family belonged to his Congregation
That said Bartholomew married her said Sister soon after he
left the army and lived with her as his Wife untill his Death
which was on 12th of December 1840 and she is now his Widow

Sworn to & subscribed this 28th day
of March 1842 before me
Chs. C. Noble Justice of the peace.

Rebecca her X mark Haynes

I also certify that Rebecca Haynes whose name is subscribed
above - is a person of reputed & unquestionable truth and
veracity & is a lawful & credible witness
Chs. C. Noble Justice Peace

State of New York } ss
Otsego County }

On the [illegible] day of April 1842 personally
appeared before me [illegible] Judge of
Otsego County Court
Catharine Reed a resident of the Town of Unadilla
in Otsego County and State of New York aged
73 years who being first duly sworn according
to Law doth declare and say that she is a Sister of
Elizabeth Bartholomew of Unadilla in Otsego County
that she now lives near her said Sister and that

she now well recollects her said Sisters Marriage
to Samuel Bartholomew which took place
at her Fathers House in Waterford in Connecticut
some time in the Month of January 1784 before
Elder Zadock Darrow the Baptist Minister there
she cannot now recollect the day of the month
but it was about the Middle of January 1784 —
that she was present at the Wedding and saw
them Married by Elder Darrow — that she was
well acquainted with him — that their Family
belong^d to his Church & Congregation — she also well
recollects that her Brother Joseph Butler was the Bride
Man Groomsman and that Sally Butler was the Bride Maid

Man Groomsman and that Sally Butler was the Bride Maid
that she saw them all standing up together and Married
as aforesaid in presence of a large Company

Sworn to & subscribed
the 6th day of April
1842 before me
Hiram Kinne Judge of
Otsego County Court

Catherine [illegible]

I certify from personal
knowledge that Catharine [illegible] whose name is subscribed
above is a credible person & lawful testimony entitled to be believed
Hiram Kinne Judge of Otsego County Court

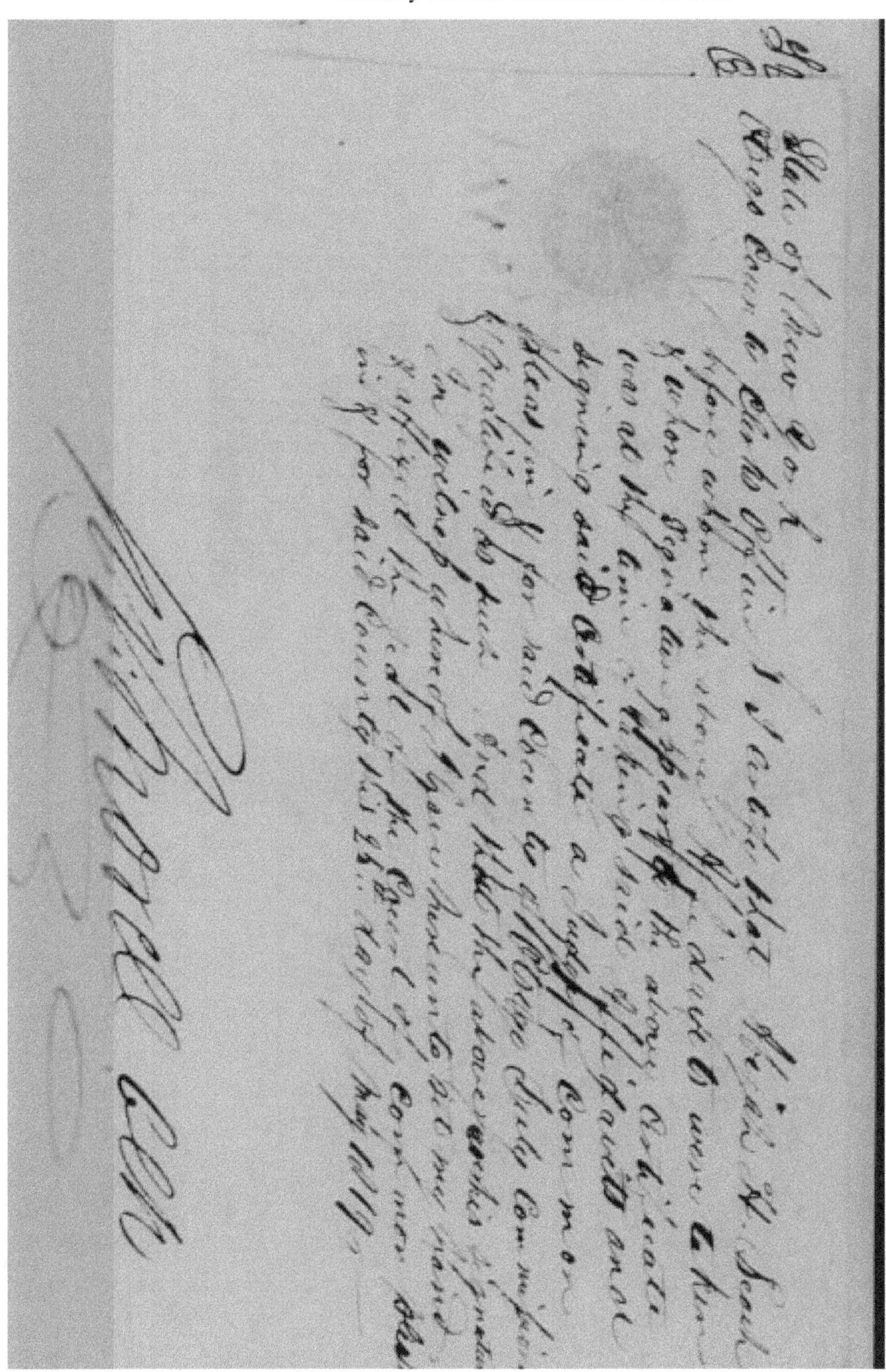

State of New York
Otsego County Clerks Office } I certify that Elijah H. Beach
before whom the above Affidavits were taken
& whose signature appears to the above certificate
was at the time of taking said Affidavits and
signing said Certificate a Judge of Common
Pleas in & for said County of Otsego duly commissioned
& qualified as such And that the above signature
In witness whereof I have hereunto set my hand
& affixed the seal of the Court of Common Pleas
in & for said County this 25th day of May 1819.

[illegible] Clk

Otsego County ss on the 20th day of April 1819 the aforesaid Jabez Maynard to me known as a Creditable person on being duly sworn further saith that he is personally well acquainted with the aforesaid Samuel Bartholomew and has been 35 years past - that he also was well acquainted with the Circumstances & recollects that the said Samuel Bartholomew served in the Army of the Revolution in the years 1781 - 1782 - & 1783 - in Colo Isaac Shermans Regt in Genl Parsons Brigade - and in the last part of the service in Colol Huntingtons Regt in Genl Huntingtons Brigade all in the Connecticut Line - that said Bartholomew was discharged from Huntingtons Regiment in the fall of the year 1783 with others

sworn & subscribed the 20 Apl 1819 before me Elijah H Beach one of the Judges as aforesaid ——

Jabez Maynard

State of New York } Otsego County ss } on the 19th day of April 1818 Jabez Maynard of the Town of Unadilla in sd County to me known personally came before me & on being duly sworn saith that he knows the above named Samuel Bartholomew and verily believes from his statement and from common report that he was in the Army of the United States and he knows some of the facts

United States and he knows some of the facts
himself & verily believes the facts set forth
in his application aforesaid to be true - and
further saith that said Bartholomew is infirm
& unable to work to support himself & family
and from his very reduced circumstances by
reason of Age and Infirmity he is in need
of assistance from his Country for support
and further saith not - Jabez Maynard

DEPARTMENT OF THE INTERIOR,

BUREAU OF PENSIONS.

Washington, D. C., ..., 19

In reply to your request of..............................., received ....
for a statement of the military history of [illegible]
a soldier of the REVOLUTIONARY WAR, you will find below the desired
information as contained in his (or his widow's) application for pe
sion on file in this Bureau.

Dates of enlistment or appointment.	Length of service.	Rank.	Officers under whom service was rendered.		State
			Captain.	Colonel.	
[illegible]	[illegible]	[illegible]	Pier[illegible]	[illegible]	
			[illegible]	[illegible]	

Battles engaged in, ...

Residence of soldier at enlistment, ...

Date of application for pension, [illegible]

Residence at date of application, [illegible]

Age at date of application, [illegible]

Remarks: [illegible]

Respectfully,

Commissioner

State of New York
Otsego County } I, William [illegible] George Morrell Clerk of the Court of Common Pleas of the County of Otsego in State of New York, do hereby certify that the foregoing oath and the schedule thereto annexed, are truly copied from the records of the said Court, and I do further certify that it is the opinion of the said Court that the total amount in value of the property exhibited in the aforesaid schedule is twenty one dollars and fifty cents.

In testimony whereof I have hereunto set my hand & affixed the seal of the said Court on the 24th day of June 1821

[illegible] Morrell Clk

State of New York }
Otsego County } ss. On the 11th day of October 1820 the aforesaid Lawrence Bartholomew personally appeared in Open Court and made oath that the above [illegible] and schedule by him subscribed are true.

Sworn this 11th Oct 1820 Before me
[illegible] Morrell Clk

his
Lawrence X Bartholomew
mark

infirm & unhealthy and can work but little my Wife
is 6[?] years old is feeble and infirm — one Son Samuel
17 years Old of feeble Constitution can work some —
One son David 2[?] years old he is helpless and speechless
and has been so from Infancy & requires Constant care
and attendance and is deprived of [illegible] and always
has been & is an Idiot

Sworn to and declared on the 6th day of
June 1820 before me

Samuel his X mark Bartholomew

Elijah H. Beach[?]
one of the Judges aforesaid

A Schedule containing the whole Real [illegible] of
Samuel Bartholomew except clothing & bedding [illegible]
together and subscribed by the said Samuel Bartholomew
before Elijah H. Beach one of the Judges of the Court of
Common Pleas at Portland on the 6th day of June 1820

Viz

One Cow one pig 3 months old four [illegible] 11.00
& [illegible] hog but one week old [illegible] 7.50
Ten old pails & one Chair 1.00
Some few articles of house hold furniture which is old and poor 2.50
$ [illegible].50

old log house [illegible] very old & miserable & not his

[illegible] in the presence of
[illegible] Thomas

Samuel his X mark Bartholomew

State of New York }
Otsego County } On the 5th day of June 1820 personally appeared before me Hezh C. Beard one of the Judges of the Court of Com. Pleas in & for said County being a Court of Record established by Law Samuel Bartholomew aged fifty seven years resident in the Town of Unadilla in the said County who being first duly sworn according to law doth on his oath declare and say that he the said Samuel Bartholomew served the United States in the Revolutionary War in the Company commanded by Capt. [illegible] and after by Capt. Stillwell in the Regiment commanded by Colonel [illegible] and after by Colonel Huntington in the Connecticut Line on the Continental Establishment. That I made application for a pension on the 13th day of April 1818 under the act of Congress passed the 18th day of March 1818. That I received a Certificate of Pension dated the 13th of June 1819 No 13.301 and I do further solemnly swear and declare that I was a resident Citizen of the United States on the 18th day of March 1818 and that I have not since that time by gift sale or in any manner whatever disposed of my property or any part thereof with intent thereby to diminish it so as to bring myself within the provisions of an act of Congress entitled an act to provide for certain persons engaged in the Land and Naval service of the United States in the Revolutionary war passed the 18th March 1818 and that I have not nor has any person in trust for me any property or securities contracts or debts due to me nor have I any income other than what is contained in the schedule hereto annexed and by me subscribed. That I am a common Laborer, [illegible]

Declaration in order to obtain the benefit of the Act of Congress of the 7th July 1838 entitled an Act granting half pay and pensions to certain Widows –

State of New York } ss
Otsego County }

On this 25th day of September 1843 Personally appeared before me Sheldon Griswold a Justice of the Peace in and for Otsego County as aforesaid – Elizabeth Bartholomew the Widow of Samuel Bartholomew (late deceased) a resident of the Town of Unadilla in the County of Otsego & State of New York Aged Eighty six years – who being first duly sworn according to Law doth on her Oath make the following Declaration in order to obtain the Benefit of the provision made by the Act of Congress passed 7th July 1838 Entitled an Act Granting half pay and pensions to certain Widows – That she is the Widow of Samuel Bartholomew who was a private soldier in Capt. [illegible] Company in Col. Huntington's Regiment in the Connecticut Line in the Revolutionary War as may fully appear of Record in the Pension Office she further declares that she was Married to the said Samuel Bartholomew on the Evening of the 13th of January 1784 at her Father's House at Waterford in Connecticut by Zadock Darrow the Baptist Minister of that place – that her Husband the aforesaid Samuel Bartholomew Died on the 12th day of December 1840 – that she was not Married to him prior to his leaving the service but the Marriage took place previous to the first of January 1794 viz at the time above stated – that she drew the arrears of his pension up to his death and surrendered his Pension Certificate – That she has not since Inter Married but has remained his Widow ever since that period and is now his Widow – It will appear by reference to her papers on file in the Pension Office at Washington that Elder Darrow who Married them kept no record of his Marriages Also that her Sisters Sally – Catherine – Rebecca & others were at the Wedding and saw them Married Affidavits on file in Pension Office &c

Sworn to and Subscribed the day & year above written before me

Sheldon Griswold
Justice of the Peace

+

Caleb Bartholomew

New York

Samuel Bartholomew

of Unadilla in the state of New York
who was a Private in the regiment commanded by
Colonel Sherman of the Connecticut
line, for the term of Three Years 1780

Inscribed on the Roll of New York
at the rate of 8 Dollars per month, to commence on
the 13 of April 1818

Certificate of Pension issued the 30 of June 1819
and sent to Abijah H. Beach Esq.
Unadilla New York

Arrears to 4th of Mar 1819 85.83
Semi-anl. all'ce ending 4 Sep 1819 48.00
$133.83

Revolutionary claim,
Act 18th March, 1818.

that he now has no further evidence in his
power of his said Services – that he is now
fifty five years of age – that he is a Resident of
the United States & of this Town – and that from
his age and Infirmities and very reduced Circum
–stances he is in Need of the Assistance of his Country
for support as aforsaid –

Sworn to Declared & Subscribed by
making his Mark on the 13th day of
April 1818 before me Abijah H–

his
Samuel R Bartholomew
Mark

The said Bartholomew further saith under Oath that he Recollects the names of Stephen Reed Thomas Rathbun — David Shipman and Thomas Kittle who served as private Soldiers in said Company Commanded by Captn Rice in Colo. Shermans Regt and that two of the Sergeants in said Company were of the name of Spencer and one of the name of Hinkley — that the Drummers name was Pixley and the fifer was David Phelps — that he does not know where either of those persons now Reside

Sworn to & subscribed as above

Samuel his X mark Bartholomew

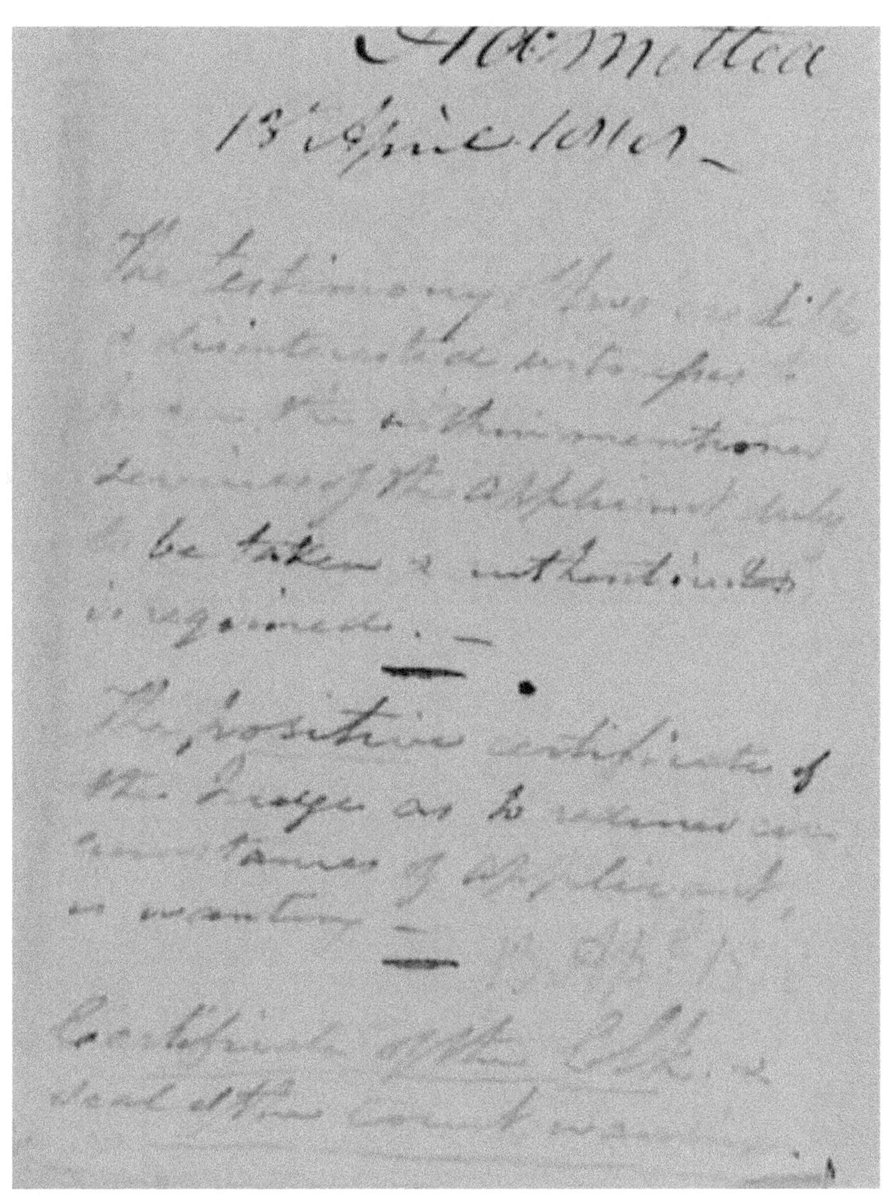

Admitted
13th April [illegible]

The testimony of [illegible] & [illegible] disinterested witnesses to prove the within mentioned services of the Applicant duly to be taken & authenticated is required. —

The positive certificate of the Judge as to reduced circumstances of Applicant is wanting —

Certificate of the Clk. & seal of the Court wanting.

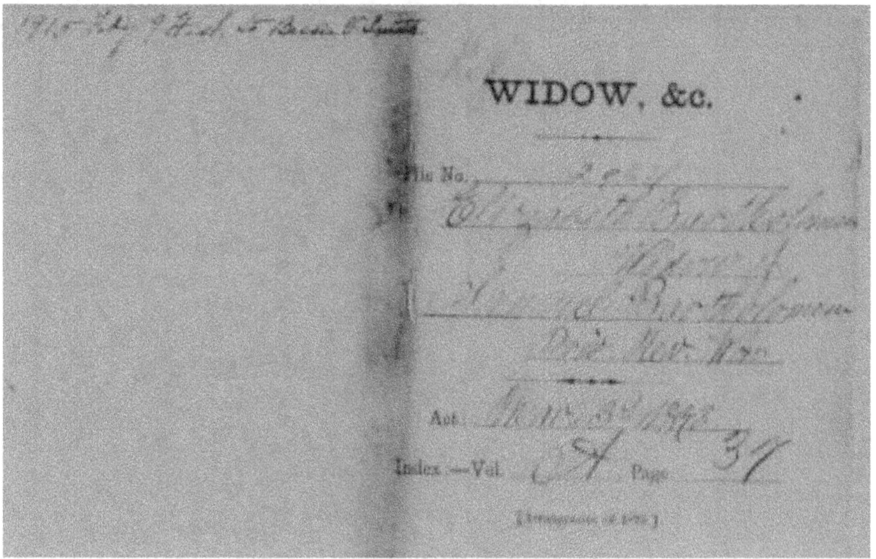

WIDOW, &c.

File No. [illegible]

[illegible]

Act. [illegible]

Index.—Vol. [illegible] Page [illegible]

his
Samuel R Bartholome
mark

in presents of —
John Willmore

sworn to by the said Samuel
Bartholemew 20th Sep. 1819
before me Elijah H Beach
a Judge of Otsego Comm Pleas

[illegible]

Unadilla Otsego County N. York
24th April 1842

Enclos'd is the application of Elizabeth Bartholomew of this place for a pension — she is a very Worthy Old Woman & has been at much expence & trouble to procure Documentary evidence of her Marriage — I have written once to the Post Master and twice to the Town Clerk of Waterford in Connecticut for such proof but it appears that no record of such Marriage was kept and that on search no record can be found either in the Town or Parish — but it appears very evident that she was Married as she represents in her statement —

Most respectfully
Your Obt Servt

Abijah H. Beach

Honl the Commissioner
of pensions — Washington

Muster Roll of Capt. Nehemiah Rice's Compy in the 5th Connecticut Regiment in Service of the United States of America commanded by Isaac Sherman Lieutenant Colonel Commandant for March and April 1781 — 76

Commissioned { November 16th 1777 Captain Nehemiah Rice
August 21st 1780 Lieutenant Joshua Whitney
January 1 1778 Ensign Isaiah Tiffany On Com. Virginia

Appointed	Serjeants	Term	Time for the Regt	Remarks
	Israel Cone			Commissary's Clerk
	Eben. Hinkley			On Com. Danbury Apl 26
	David Dixon			
	Thomas Spencer			
	Elijah Pike			On Com. Virginia Feb 7 [illegible]
	Drum			
	Elijah Rexle			
Enlisted	Privates			
Jan 18 78	Saml Bartholomew	3 years	April 6 81	
Feb 13 81	Jeremiah Booth	Do	do 25	On Duty
	David Brown	Do	do 6	
Jan 4th	Bethel Camp	Do	do 2	On Duty
	Daniel Cone	Do	9	On Duty
	Eli Denslow			
Jan 15th	Caesar Doolittle	Do	Apl 2	
	Thomas Earl			On Command Virginia [illegible]
	George Fields			On Com. Danbury
	James Griffin			with the [illegible]
	Levi Hitchcock			
Jan 14	Roswell Hotchkiss	3 years	Apl 2	
	Prince Hotchkiss			
	Pomp London			Sick N Hampshire [illegible]
Feb 12th	John Marney	Do	March 6	
	Samuel Mitchel			Baker N Hampshire [illegible]

Appointed	Corporals	Term	Time for the Regt	Remarks
	Amos Clark			
	John Daboll			
	Moses Culver			On Com. Virginia Feb 7 1781
	Fife			
	David Phelps			
Enlisted	Privates			
	Daniel Munrow			On Com. Virginia Feb 17th 81
	John Marsh			On Duty
March 11 78	John McMannors			time expired March 11th 1781
	Jesse Matthews			
	Isaiah Moss			On Com. Fredericksburg [illegible]
	Zachariah Rolo			Waggoner
Dec 25 80	Humphrey Potter	3 years	Apl 2 81	
Jan 3 81	James Prout	Do	2	
	Stephen Reed	Do	6	
	Ethel Scott			
Jan 27	George W. Shipman	Do	Apl 6th	
	Simeon Taylor			Black Smith
	Joshua Fox			Discharged Apl 5 1781
	Saml C. Heath			Deserted Jan 16th 81
	Warrick Ray			Transferred Invalid Corps April 7

May 1781 Mustered then Capt. Rice's Compy as specified in the above Roll —

Warner Sub Inspector [illegible] Brigade

her Husband having died in 1840 – we see no reason
why she was not then allowed from his Death to 1841 – and
we see no reason now why she agreeable to present regu-
=lations she is not entitled to the five years from 1836 to
1841 as others are — her papers are in the Pension Office
and she wishes you to examine them and let us know
the result –

Most respectfully
Your Obt Servt
Abijah H. Beach

Hon. J. L. Edwards
Comr of Pensions

Caleb Bartholomew

Saml. Bartholomew
Priv.

Col. Sherman's
Connecticut Regt.

86 to 83

1779 —

Admitted
13 April 1818 —

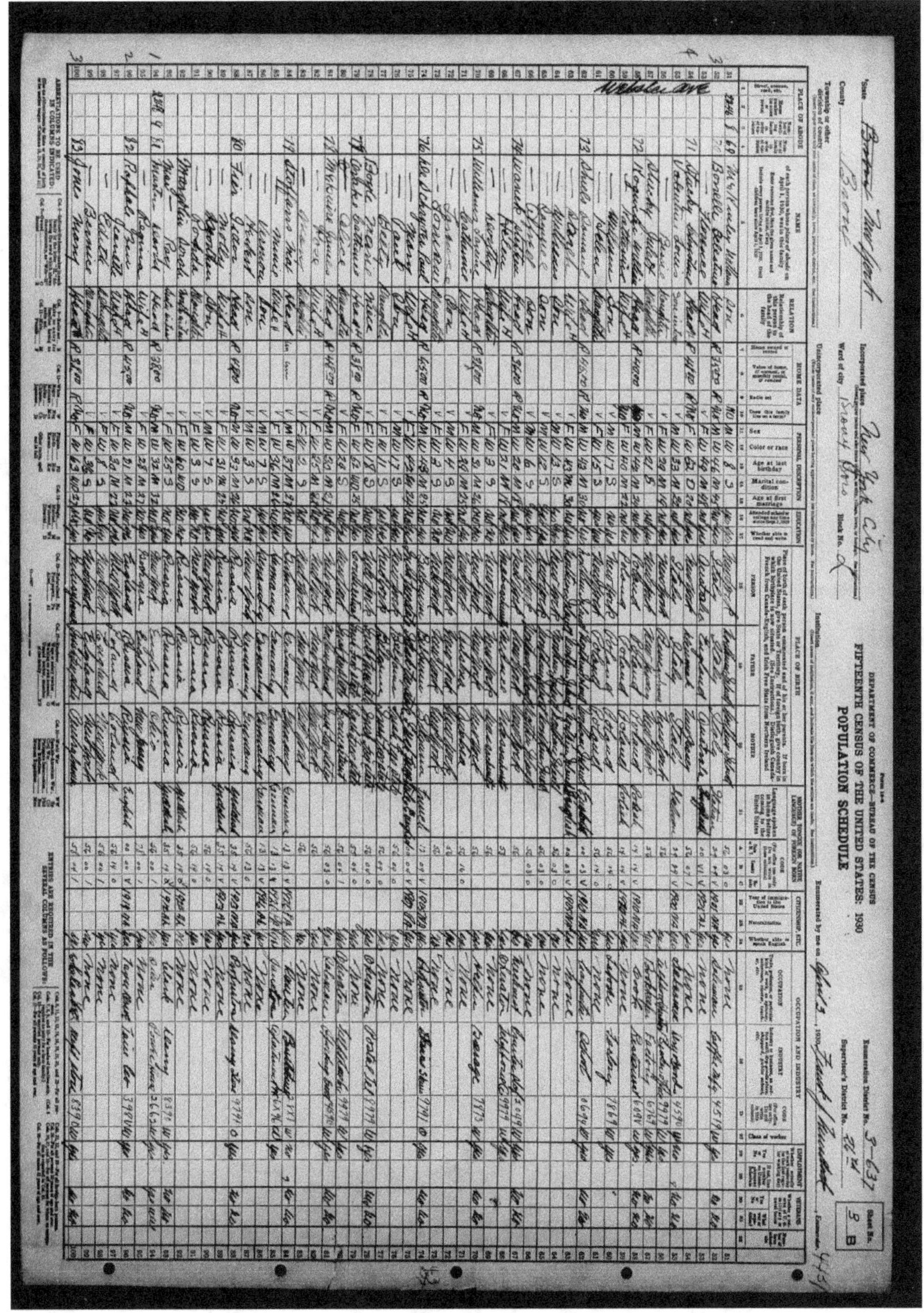

DEPARTMENT OF COMMERCE—BUREAU OF THE CENSUS
FIFTEENTH CENSUS OF THE UNITED STATES: 1930
POPULATION SCHEDULE

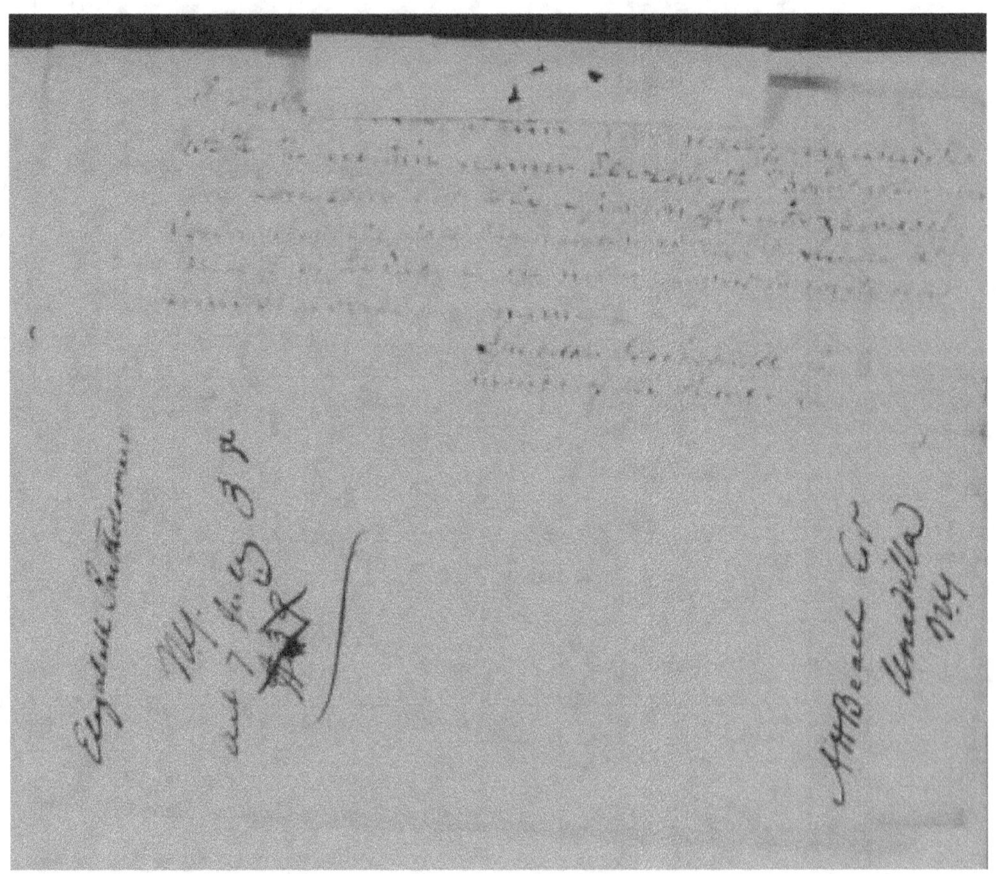

8016

New York

Albany

Elizabeth Bartholomew

widow of Samuel Bartholomew

$400.00

[Act July 7, 1838.]

Recorded by [illegible] Clerk,

Book [illegible] Vol. 1 Page 149

Roll & Muster of the 2 Company Connecticut Regiment, Commanded by Col. Heman Swift For the Month of September 1783 —

Rank	Names	Term of Enlistment	Casualties	Mustered	Time since last Muster	Alterations since last Muster
Capt.	Elias Stilwell	July 79		— Stilwell	2 Sept. 1783	
Lieut.	Jeshua Whitney	20 Aug 80		— Whitney	D°	
Serjt.	Ezra Sibley	3 Months		— Sibley	2 Sept. 83	
—	Abial Farnham	4 D°		— Farnham	D°	
—	Frederick Sterre	3 D°		— Sterre	D°	
Corpl.	Benjamin Treadwell	3 Months		— Treadwell	2 Sept. 83	
—	Elihu Dodge	3 D°		— Dodge	D°	
—	Preserved Redway	5 D°		— Redway	D°	
Fife	Isaac Higgins	5 Months		—	2 Sept. 83	Transferred to Capt. Cuyler's Comp. 7 from the last Muster
Private	Stephen Bennet	2 Months		— Bennet	2 Sept. 83	
2	Israel Clarke	3 D°		— Clarke	D°	
3	Sage Churchell	2 D°		— Churchell	D°	
4	David Butler	6 D°		— Butler	D°	
5	Reuben Chapman	3 D°		— Chapman	D°	
6	George Harriss	4 D°		— Harriss	D°	
7	Luther Grover	5 D°		L — Grover	D°	
8	Jehiel Wilcox	4 D°		— Wilcox	D°	
9	Amasa Grover	5 D°		A — Grover	D°	
10	Clement Carr	3 D°		— Carr	D°	
11	Elijah Randoll	2 D°		— Randoll	D°	
12	John Whitman	3 D°		— Whitman	D°	
13	Israel Ransom	4 D°		— Ransom	D°	
14	Thos. Bishop	2 D°		— Bishop	D°	
15	Moses Tracy	4 D°		— Tracy	D°	
16	Daniel Snyder	3 D°		— Snyder	D°	
17	Solomon Woodruff	2 D°		— Woodruff	D°	
18	Worth Armstrong	8 D°		— Armstrong	D°	
19	Timothy Woodbridge	2 D°		— Woodbridge	D°	
20	Ebenezer Brown	3 D°		E — Brown	D°	
21	Thos. Rathbun	4 D°		— Rathbun	D°	
22	Asa Geer	6 D°		— Geer	D°	
23	Saml. Bartholomew	3 D°		— Bartholomew	D°	
24	Meritt Elderkin	2 D°		— Elderkin	D°	
25	Jonathan Gaylor	2 D°		— Gaylor	D°	
26	Jesse Shepherd	2 D°		— Shepherd	D°	
27	Isaac Wardwell	3 D°		— Wardwell	D°	
28	Samuel Lane	3 D°		— Lane	D°	
29	Thos. Dinsmore	20 D°		— Dinsmore	D°	
30	Nathaniel Clarke	4 D°		N — Clarke	D°	
31	Simon Cummins	4 D°		— Cummins	D°	
32	Jonathan Brown	3 D°		J — Brown	D°	
33	Tuis Sharper	6 D°		— Sharper	D°	
34	Ceasar Beaumont	3 D°		— Beaumont	D°	
35	Dick Bristor	3 D°		— Bristor	D°	
36	Juba Dyer	4 D°		— Dyer	D°	
37	Peter Beguiree	3 D°		— Beguiree	D°	
—	James Hall	8 D°		—	D°	Deserted 14th of Sept. 1783
—	Stephen Bristol	3 D°		—	D°	D° 10 Sept. 83
—	Asa Sawyer	7 D°		—	D°	D° 14 Sept. 83
—	Thos. Manning	4 D°		—	D°	D° 14 Sept. 83

I Certify the above Roll to be the true State of the Company This 14th day of October 1783 —

E. Stilwell Capt.

I Certify the above to be true in all its Contents Inspection of September 1783

W. Barber Major &
Asst. Inspector of the northern Army

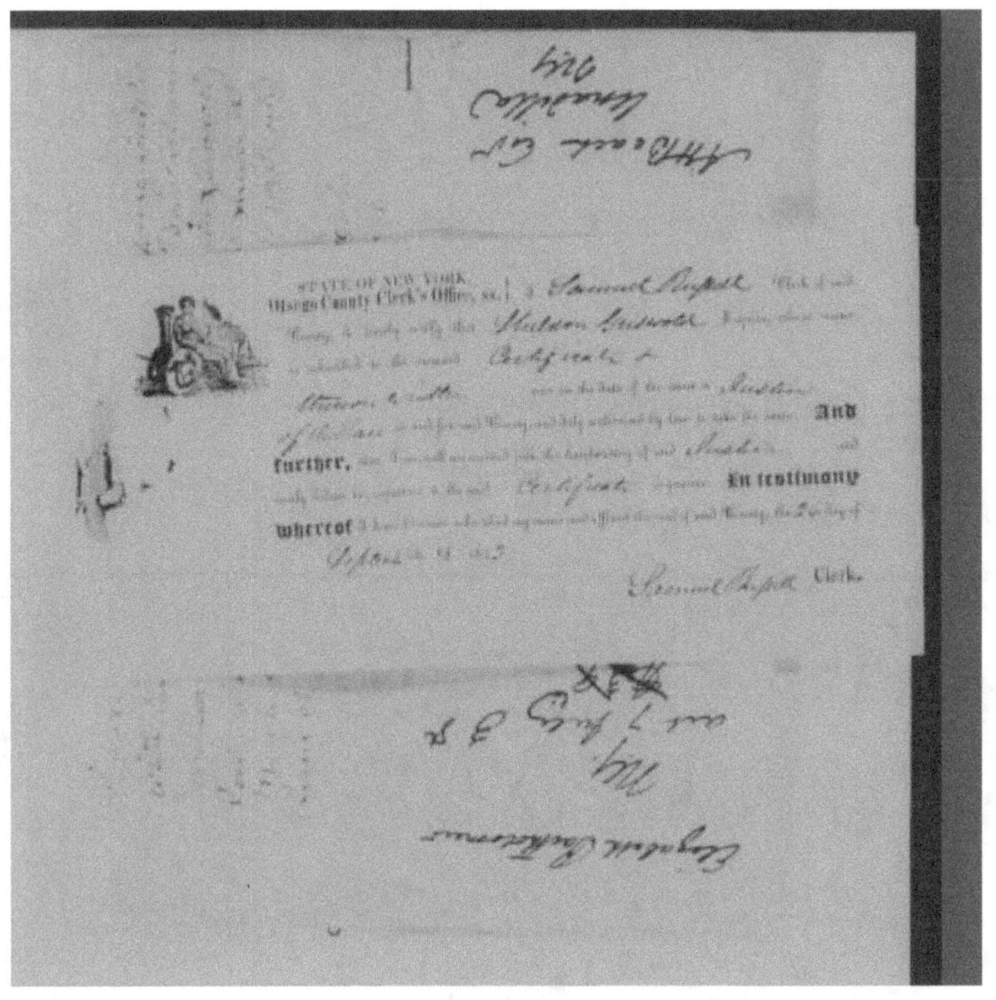
STATE OF NEW YORK,
Otsego County Clerk's Office, ss.

And further,

In testimony whereof

Clerk.

Caleb Bartholomew

State of New York }
Otsego County ss }

on the 20th April 1819 John Wellman and Chedor L. Collins both known to me the subscriber to be Creditable persons and on being duly sworn doth each for himself depose and say – that they were in the Army of the Revolution in the years 1781 – 1782 – and 1783 – that they were both at West Point in State of New York some part of the time in those three years. and with the Army Constantly – that they both are well acquainted with the aforesaid Samuel Bartholomew and with each other – that they are perfectly well Satisfied and verely believe that the said Samuel Bartholomew did serve in the said Army in those three years – at West Point and in other places with them in the said Army – for they well Recollect many Circumstances which took place with them in those three Campaigns and in Winter quarters when they all three were in said Army

Sworn to & Subscribed on the 20th day of April 1819 before me Abijah H Beach one of the Judges of Otsego County }

John Wellman
Chedor L Collins

State of New York
Otsego County Clerks Office ss. I George Morell
Clerk of the Court of Common Pleas
of the County of Otsego aforesaid being
a court of Record, do hereby certify
that the within named Samuel Barthol
omew personally appeared in open Court
on the 11th October 1820 & took and
subscribed the within affidavit

In testimony whereof I have
hereunto set my hand & affixed
the seal of the said Court this 11th October
1820

G. Morell Clk

of the Judges aforesaid

Otsego County ss

20th April
1819

I hereby certify of my own knowledge that
the aforesaid Samuel Bartholomew is
infirm and in very Indigent circumstances
and I am fully satisfied that he absolutely
needs the assistance of his Country for
Support —

Elijah H Beach one
of the Judges of Otsego County

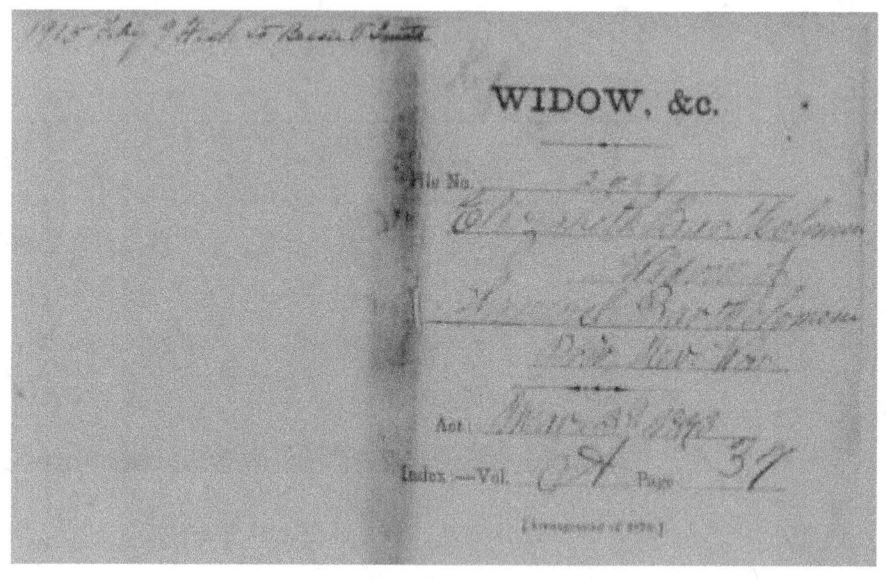
WIDOW, &c.

File No.

Act:

Index:—Vol. Page

Chauncey Bartholomew had three sons. The other two are worth honorable mention because of their acts of valor in the United States Civil War.

Alfred was Chauncey's middle son. He fought with the famous New York 121st infantry regiment. The 121st claims they caught Custis Lee, Robert E Lee's son, in Virginia but so does the 37th infantry in Massachusetts. It is still in dispute and the Army is still investigating to this day[100]

The 121st was organized out of Otsego county, and called the Onsers or Upton's Regulars and they were mustered into the Union Army in 1862. The (Bartlett's) 2nd Brigade, (Brooke's) 1st Division, 6th Corp, 121st Company F, Unadilla, fought in Fredericksburg but not direct combat and in the battle at Gettysburg as a reserve unit but even as reserve they still had casualties. They also engaged lightly at Rappahannock and Mine Run but did not fully engage until after they assisted General Grant in crossing the Rapidan River.[101][102]

On May 4th, 1864 General Grant, who had just taken control of the Union Army, embarked on a move that would change the landscape of the Civil War and decide the fate. They crossed the Rapidan River at that time and while they did not fight a battle that day, they sat poised against two Confederate Generals, but General Lee and General Joseph Johnston. Grant commanded Sherman to engage Johnston.

Grant crossed the river and encamped with 100,000 Union soldiers, inside the Wilderness forest. The game plan was to have the Federal Army to

---

[100] https://en.m.wikipedia.org/wiki/121st_New_York_Infantry

[101] Ibid

[102]

https://dmna.ny.gov/historic/reghist/civil/infantry/121stInf/121stInfMain.htm 2017

flank left on the other side of the Wilderness but the forest was too thick and slowed the advancements down. The numbers the Union presented were diminished due to the entanglement in the Wilderness. On April 5th the battle of the Wilderness began.[103]This is where most records say Alfred lost his life but some say he died at Spotsylvania, which is where the left flank was supposed to converge. Either case it was within a couple of days within the same geographical location. Based on consistent dates given it was more likely than not at Spotsylvania

---

[103] http://www.history.com/this-day-in-history/army-of-the-potomac-crosses-the-rapidan

content.com/pod-product-compliance
LLC

26
05B/731